Bias-aware Teaching, Learning and Assessment

CRITICAL PRACTICE IN HIGHER EDUCATION

Acknowledgements

We would like to thank colleagues who participated in the coaching dialogues and who kindly agreed to share them through this book. Thanks to their contributions this book is rooted in current higher education practice, and colleagues' professional insights and reflections provide alternative perspectives on bias-aware practices. We are also indebted to our academic editors, Joy and Karen, who saw potential in our proposal and contributed to the book's development through their thorough feedback and ongoing encouragement. And finally, thank you to all the colleagues who have inspired us to write this book and whose inclusive practices have informed the practical, bias-aware strategies offered in each chapter.

To order, or for details of our bulk discounts, please go to our website www.criticalpublishing.com or contact our distributor, Ingram Publisher Services (IPS UK), 10 Thornbury Road, Plymouth PL6 7PP, telephone 01752 202301 or email IPSUK.orders@ingramcontent.com

Bias-aware Teaching, Learning and Assessment

Donna Hurford and Andrew Read

Series Editors: Joy Jarvis and Karen Smith

CRITICAL PRACTICE IN HIGHER EDUCATION

First published in 2022 by Critical Publishing Ltd

British Library Cataloguing in Publication Data
A CIP record for this book is available from the British Library

ISBN: 9781914171895

This book is also available in the following e-book formats:
EPUB ISBN: 9781914171901
Adobe e-book ISBN: 9781914171918

Cover design by Out of House Limited
Text design by Greensplash Limited
Project management by Newgen Publishing UK
Printed and bound in Great Britain by 4edge, Essex

Critical Publishing
3 Connaught Road
St Albans
AL3 5RX

www.criticalpublishing.com

Printed on FSC accredited paper

Contents

Meet the authors and series editors

Donna Hurford has worked as an academic developer at the University of Southern Denmark since 2013 where she leads the Lecturer Training Programme, teaches and offers consultancy on among other topics collaborative learning, addressing bias, integrating SDGs, assessment and questioning. Coming from a background in school teaching and later pre-service education at the University of Cumbria, UK her interest in assessment for learning became the focus of her PhD. After years seeking and exploiting opportunities to address inclusive education through global citizenship and internationalising the curriculum in HE teaching, Donna sees addressing bias as fundamental to inclusive education.

Andrew Read taught in primary schools in east London, UK, from 1990 to 2005. From 2005 to 2021 he worked as a university lecturer in the field of Education. From 2010 to 2016 he was Head of Primary Teacher Education at the University of East London. In 2016 Andrew moved to London South Bank University and was Head of the Education Division there from 2018. In 2021 Andrew became an independent educational consultant. Andrew is particularly interested in assessment, stemming from his experience of working with pupils from disadvantaged backgrounds and non-traditional students in HE.

Joy Jarvis is currently Professor of Educational Practice at the University of Hertfordshire and a UK National Teaching Fellow. She has experience in a wide range of education contexts and works to create effective learning experiences for students and colleagues. She is particularly interested in the professional learning of those engaged in educational practice in HE settings and has undertaken a range of projects, working with colleagues locally, nationally and internationally, to develop practice in teaching and leadership of teaching. Joy works with doctoral students exploring aspects of educational practice and encourages them to be adventurous in their methodological approaches and to share their findings in a range of contexts to enable practice change.

 **Karen Smith** is Reader in Higher Education in the School of Education at the University of Hertfordshire. Her research focuses on how higher education policies and practices impact on those who work and study within universities. Karen has worked within educational development and on lecturer development programmes. She holds a Principal Fellowship of the Higher Education Academy and is currently the Director of the University of Hertfordshire's Professional Doctorate in Education. Karen also leads collaborative research and development in her School, where she engages in externally funded research and evaluation and supports the development of scholarly educational practice through practitioner research.

Book summary

We know that bias is prevalent in higher education (HE) and believe that developing bias-aware practice represents a significant step towards inclusive HE. We also know that dialogue is an effective tool for unpicking meanings and assumptions, and believe this can be applied effectively to the process of developing bias-aware practice. We wrote this book to share our ideas for employing dialogue to raise awareness and address bias in HE at institutional and strategic levels, and through teaching, learning and assessment. The chapters include coaching dialogues in which HE professionals consider aspects of HE pedagogy or institutional practice. These dialogues reflect the diversity of the participants and the chapter topics. The coachees were invited to contribute a dialogue to this book; however, they were not asked to explicitly discuss bias in HE. Instead, they were asked to reflect on particular HE experiences and to allow the coach to facilitate critical reflection. Coaching models, like the GROW model which we employed in this book, provide scaffolds for focused conversations and serve to professionalise dialogue. We believe that the GROW model provides a flexible scaffold that the coach can adapt to best suit the flow of each dialogue and facilitate critical reflection by both coach and coachee. Through sensitive analysis of the coaching dialogues, we raise awareness of different biases and their effects on perceptions, interactions, attitudes and behaviours and offer practical ways forward. The chapters conclude with collections of inclusive strategies which HE practitioners can employ to address the biases highlighted in the dialogues or at least mitigate their effects and contribute to bias-free and inclusive HE.

Why this book?

The rationale of this book is to provoke awareness of how conscious and unconscious biases can influence interactions, teaching, learning and assessment at higher education institutions (HEIs), and how bias at an institutional level is manifested. We go on to share practical and inclusive strategies that higher education (HE) teachers, module and course leaders and those in leadership positions can use to address bias from an individual to an institution-wide level.

The words 'bias' and 'biased' are often used unthinkingly, spontaneously and perhaps with the aim to close down an argument, or to cast another person in a negative light. How often have you thought, or said, *'You're so biased'* or *'That's so biased'*? We recognise imbalance or prejudice in others, but we don't always recognise it in ourselves. In this book, our aim is not only to take bias seriously, but also to acknowledge that bias is something we all have, and for which we all have responsibility.

We know biases, both conscious and unconscious, influence judgements, perceptions, decision-making and actions; this is nothing new (Tversky and Kahneman, 1974). We may rely on our biases particularly when we are time-pressed and under pressure. They trigger our expedient responses and thereby simplify complexity, but this expediency comes at a cost. Kahneman (2011) differentiates between *'System One'*, our expedient, unconscious responses, and *'System Two'*, our conscious, critical thinking. He explains how when we allow our emotional *'System One'* to dictate our responses, we are foregoing our critical *'System Two'*, which would enable us to craft a more considered response. A considered response may of course still be biased, but unlike *'System One'* it affords us the option to address or at least mitigate the impact of our biases (Kahneman, 2011).

Knowing what we do about bias and its potential impact in order to achieve inclusion, equity and equality of opportunity, we have to recognise and effectively address individual and structural biases. One-off unconscious bias training is rarely recommended, and it is hard to know which approaches are effective for addressing bias and its impact, especially in contexts where people are time-pressed and managing diverse roles and responsibilities (Atewologun et al, 2018; Noon, 2018).

When planning this book, we applied Benson's (2016) codex of cognitive biases which could potentially affect interaction, learning activities, course design and curriculum, assessment and institutional structures at HEIs. Benson's (2016) 'Cognitive Bias Codex' has proved to be an informative and reliable resource, with its clear references to hundreds of cognitive biases, loosely distributed into four categories, namely: too much information – when we choose the easiest option and thereby miss out on nuance and thoroughness; not enough meaning – when we don't understand something and we draw on what we think we know rather than checking for facts; need to act fast – when we prioritise expediency and risk forgoing accuracy and thoroughness; what should we remember? – when we rely on memory rather than checking current information (Benson, 2016). In Table 1.1 on page 5, we present one or more biases for each of these four categories and indicate in which chapter they will be introduced. To illustrate how these biases come into play, each chapter includes its own coaching dialogue, using coaching questions based on the GROW coaching model (Whitmore, 2017). By analysing the dialogues, we reveal how different cognitive biases can influence perceptions, practices and decisions. We present some of these findings as critical issues and offer them to you for further contemplation, with particular regard to your own HE contexts. The chapters conclude with lists of approaches or strategies for addressing the relevant biases or at least mitigating their negative effects.

Why write it collaboratively and why us?

We have taught at the same HEI and have continued to work collaboratively on a number of scholarship of teaching and learning (SOTL) projects. These have often involved working remotely, using a range of online collaborative tools and platforms. Currently, one of us is based in Denmark, the other in the UK. While Covid-19 has impacted on our on-campus in-person practice, we have been able to continue working collaboratively online as we have tended to for the last 12 years. Collaboration offers the opportunity to share and challenge assumptions and thinking and suggest alternative perspectives. This is particularly relevant in the content of writing about bias and biases. While writing this book, we have been particularly watchful that our long-term collaboration may lead to groupthink bias (see Chapter 4). We have attempted to address this by sharing the tasks, then reflecting critically on each other's work. Over time, we have built a trusting and trustful working relationship, where we feel safe critiquing each other's writing. Having said this, we recognise that we have chosen to continue to work together because of our common values and interests: we acknowledge 'the bubble' that exists. We have further relied on feedback on drafted work from dialogue participants, as well as feedback from Karen and Joy, our academic editors.

Who is this book for?

We hope that this book is of interest to all those working in HE with a commitment to social justice. We anticipate that lecturers with teaching and supervision roles, course leaders and managers will find the content relevant and will perhaps see themselves and those they work with represented in the dialogues and other scenarios. We believe that the book will prompt those who read it to identify and act on the agency they have to positively develop practice and influence institutional strategies and policies. This book is designed to complement the guides for addressing systemic institutional bias in the HEI sector (Amos and Doku, 2019a, 2019b).

Why coaching dialogues and why this structure?

Dialogue is central to our experience as collaborative researchers and writers. Dialogue unearths hidden ideas and assumptions; dialogue is a tool to sound out and nego-tiate potential solutions. Dialogue seemed like a familiar everyday canvas on which to explore the knotty landscape of bias and biases. But we sought a particular model for these dialogues to provide a sense of consistency within the book. We turned to the GROW coaching model (Whitmore, 2017) because of its simple structure, and because it may be familiar to those who have coached or been coached. The GROW model proceeds through the sequence below.

>> G – goal, eg 'What do you want to take away from this coaching session?'

>> R – reality, eg 'What resources do you currently have available?'

>> O – options, eg 'How could you address this problem?'

>> W – wrap up, eg 'What will you do next?'

We applied the British Educational Research Association's (BERA, 2019) guidance on ethical participation. All of the dialogues involved academics working in HE and took place online, using either Zoom or Teams as a communication platform. From our first contact with potential participants, we made our intention to write a book exploring bias explicit. Before completing a dialogue, we informed the dialogue participants of our intention to use the edited content of the dialogue in our proposed book, gaining verbal consent to continue. We invited the participants to review the relevant draft chapter and ensured that we had their written consent by email before proceeding to publication. We recorded each dialogue, with participant consent (and in some cases with participant facilitation), then transcribed the recorded dialogue and edited it.

We have used aliases for the names of all participants other than in Chapter 4, where the dialogue is between the authors, Andrew and Donna. We edited the dialogues in order to remove language, such as institutional-specific terminology, or other content which might indicate the participants' identities or specific institutions. We also edited the dialogues where necessary for the purposes of chapter length, removing parts of the dialogue which we felt were less relevant or which duplicated content which we felt was already covered.

The dialogues are sometimes messy: they don't always follow the GROW model precisely. In some dialogues elements of the GROW model are omitted, and in some elements are repeated. We would argue that this is the nature of dialogue: imperfect, flexible, illogical and, sometimes, revelatory.

What is this book about?

When planning the book, we identified a number of biases that we expected to find. We identified where we thought particular biases would be clearest or most prevalent within HEIs and sorted these biases into categories – such as 'assessment' and 'interactions' – which later became chapters. Of course, in anticipating certain biases and categorising them in certain ways we were demonstrating the biases present in our own thinking. Table 1.1 provides an overview of the biases as discussed in each chapter; each bias includes a short illustration of how it could manifest in HE interaction. Each bias is then explained more fully in the chapters indicated below.

Some of the biases that we anticipated emerge in the dialogues. In some cases, participants in the dialogues are already aware of particular biases, and the dialogue revolves around how these biases are challenged. In other cases, the biases are evident, but not, perhaps, to the participants. We invite readers to inhabit the participants' shoes: we could ask ourselves if we had ever felt or voiced this type of thinking.

If we think of education as a variety of ways in which teachers and learners interact in order to facilitate learning, it is perhaps unsurprising how some biases revealed themselves in more than one chapter. Hence, we have revisited certain cognitive biases including different forms of stereotyping, the bias blind spot, the IKEA effect and the status quo bias in more than one chapter, while others such as the planning fallacy bias and the authority bias are only discussed in specific chapters.

Table 1.1 Overview of biases and in which chapters they are introduced.

Chapter	Cognitive Bias Codex (Benson, 2016)			
	1: Too much information	**2: Not enough meaning**	**3: Need to act fast**	**4: What should we remember?**
2: Interactions	Bias blind spot: 'The judgements of others are impaired, but not mine'	Explicit and implicit stereotyping, including: group attribution: 'All male students …' In-group bias: students favouring own gender or ethnicity Confirmation bias: 'I expect students to be able to …'	IKEA effect: 'My presentation is more important than my engagement with others' work' Law of the instrument: 'I've always taught this topic in a 3-hour lecture'	
3: Course design and content		Authority bias: 'She's got a PhD – she knows what she's talking about' Stereotyping: 'This is what students at this university are like'	Status quo bias: 'This is how things work here'	
4: Learning activities	Conformist groupthink: 'I agree with everyone else in the group'	Planning fallacy bias: 'It won't take us long to complete this' In-group bias: 'Let's work together because we think in the same way'	Law of triviality: participants spend more time on less rather than more complex tasks – because complex tasks require more information and time	
5: Assessment	Confirmation bias: 'I thought this would be the case, and this only goes to show that I was correct'	Halo effect: 'I like that student – he's bound to do well' Curse of knowledge: 'I don't get why students don't understand what I mean' Functional fixedness: 'This is how this resource should be used'	IKEA effect: 'It took me ages to write this assignment so it must be worth a higher grade'	

→

Table 1.1 (*Cont.*)

Chapter	Cognitive Bias Codex (Benson, 2016)			
	1: Too much information	**2: Not enough meaning**	**3: Need to act fast**	**4: What should we remember?**
6: Structural and institutional biases	Bias blind spot: 'Other institutions fail in this respect, but not us'		Stereotyping: 'This is what first-in-family students need' IKEA effect: 'Students will have put a lot of work into this assignment – the grade should reflect this' Status quo bias: 'We don't use the full spectrum of marks here'	Stereotype threat bias: 'He still looks like the best fit for the role'
7: Addressing interconnecting biases	Conformist groupthink: 'We've all made this clear to students'	Functional fixedness: 'This worked when we taught on campus so it should work when we move online' Curse of knowledge: 'It's clear to me, so it should be clear to students'	Stereotyping: 'Students behave like this because they're all ...' IKEA effect: 'I've set these activities up, so they should work' Status quo bias: 'I don't want to rock the boat'	

In Chapter 2, 'Interactions', Daniel invites Jonas, a relatively new teacher, to share how he addressed his students' initial cursory interest in their peers' course presentations. Daniel concludes that Jonas orchestrated student engagement in such a way that they had to engage with their bias blind spot towards the value of their peers' presentations and challenge their own tendency for an IKEA effect preference for their own efforts. In turn, the dialogue reveals how expectation bias can be used positively.

Next we turn to Chapter 3, 'Course design and content, where due to Mary's explicit academic engagement with status quo bias and authority bias, Rob applies a light-touch GROW coaching model. Mary shares how she encourages students to challenge their assumptions and to be critically aware of the pervasive effect of status quo bias in educational and societal systems. In recognition of how students can adopt an authority bias towards her expert researcher status, Mary provokes their critical thinking through her use of images and analogies to help students visualise alternative perspectives.

Moving on to Chapter 4, 'Learning activities', Andrew coaches Donna through her critical reflections on a particular learning activity on global citizenship from a course they had both taught more than a decade earlier. Here the pair suggest how biases like planning fallacy, the law of triviality and the IKEA effect may have influenced student perceptions of the learning activity. But what is even more revelatory is how through the coaching dialogue, Donna identifies her own unconscious assumptions and biases which influenced her design of the learning activity.

Chapter 5, 'Assessment', is the last chapter that specifically targets HE teachers. Here, Ulla is coached by Jack. Ulla's tacit knowledge about a module and her expectations of the students' understanding of the module assessment is explained by the curse of knowledge bias which disables experts from recognising novices' position. Biases often coexist and reinforce each other, such as the interplay in this example between curse of knowledge and functional fixedness, which manifests itself when we have established routines and approaches and we can't imagine other ways to do things.

In Chapter 6, 'Structural and institutional biases', we shift the focus away from the individual teacher and address bias in their modules and courses to the institutional context, where systemic biases are prone to affect us all. Here Sanne coaches Faisal, a senior academic manager, and together they unpack the covert nature of status quo bias, confirmation bias and bias blind spot, all of which are found to impact on institutional identity, staff perceptions of students and institutional assessment procedures.

In Chapter 7, 'Addressing interconnecting biases', we conclude the book by focusing on the challenges which accompany course leadership through a short dialogue between Pete and Sue. The dialogue highlights the complexity which besets a course leader when addressing issues raised in student evaluations. We see how a variety of interconnected biases including stereotyping, the IKEA effect, bias blind spot and status quo bias can influence course leadership. The book concludes with strategies for addressing bias in HEIs at all levels and by all who have agency to effect social justice.

A note on terminology

The terminology which HEIs use to describe what is delivered is not universal. One HEI might describe a three-year undergraduate experience leading to the award of a degree as 'a programme', another HEI might describe this as 'a course'. One credit-bearing component of this experience might be labelled 'a course' at one HEI and 'a module' at another. Throughout this book, we use the term 'course' to describe a combination of elements leading to an award, and the term 'module' to describe one credit-bearing component of that course.

A note on our approach to referencing

The references in this book include authors' full names. By sharing authors' first and given names, we are raising awareness of and promoting author diversities. HE course reading lists are repeatedly found to be dominated by western, male authors (Tange and Millar, 2016) with an under-representation of female authors (Harris et al, 2020; Phull et al, 2019) and limited representation of HE student diversity (Schucan Bird and Pitman, 2020). In response, we have adopted a recommendation for raising awareness of some diversities by including *'full citations for readings on syllabi'* (Harris et al, 2020, p 12). However, in view of the limitations of this approach – including full names does not accommodate gender diversities beyond traditional cisgender naming, nor does it signal the heritage of an author – Chapter 3 offers further strategies and resources for addressing bias in course curricula.

Critical questions for practice

» How important is it to identify and address bias?

» Who has the responsibility to identify address bias in our courses?

» What systems are in place in our institutions to identify and address bias?

Summary

- Conscious and unconscious biases can influence interactions, teaching, learning and assessment in HE.

- Coaching dialogues provide a supportive structure for identifying biases and crafting strategies to address them.

Useful texts

Atewologun, Doyin; **Cornish**, Tinu and **Tresh**, Fatima (2018) Unconscious Bias Training: An Assessment of the Evidence for Effectiveness. Equality and Human Rights Commission, UK. [online] Available at: www.equalityhumanrights.com/ sites/default/files/research-report-113-unconcious-bais-training-an-assessment-of-the-evidence-for-effectiveness-pdf.pdf (accessed 12 January 2022).

This report reveals how addressing bias is more complex than one-off unconscious bias training and instead provides a useful checklist for addressing bias in HE with sustained effect.

Benson, Buster (2016) Cognitive Bias Codex. [online] Available at: https://busterben son.com/piles/cognitive-biases/ (accessed 12 January 2022).

The diagrammatic categorisation of hundreds of cognitive biases into four broad categories can help identify when and where we are most likely to experience different biases.

Kahneman, Daniel (2011) *Thinking, Fast and Slow*. London: Penguin.

Kahneman's Nobel Prize-winning research into bias is shared in this accessible and compelling read about how bias is manifested in HE even when we think we have trained ourselves to be critical thinkers.

Introduction

In this chapter we explore bias in teacher–student and student–student interactions, with a particular emphasis on verbal interaction. In the opening theoretical background section, we grapple with how perceptions affect our interactions. We reflect on the implications of the preference for active learning and student participation expressed by HEIs, especially western HEIs. While acknowledging the pedagogic opportunities associated with interactive learning, we share a more circumspect perspective, which reveals how expectations of student interaction may limit perceptions of students as effective and engaged learners. We touch on how the design of group work tasks can influence the quality of student–student interaction, although course design is more generally explored in Chapter 3. Moving between the nexus of theory and practice, we analyse a GROW (Whitmore, 2017) coaching dialogue. The GROW model is described and explained in Chapter 1. In the coaching dialogue, shown later in this chapter, Daniel asks Jonas about an approach he has employed to increase student interactions in a Danish HEI. The analysis of the coaching dialogue provides an opportunity to identify and categorise examples of cognitive biases or potential biases and illustrates how flexible use of the four-stage coaching model can support a collegial, open dialogue. Following the analysis, we offer six practical ways to prevent or mitigate bias in teacher–student and student–student interactions. Many of the approaches are interconnected with ones we advocate in the other chapters, especially Course Design and Learning Activities. And as chapter take-aways, we offer three critical questions, a summary of key points and three recommended sources, all of which could help initiate a discussion with colleagues on addressing bias in interaction.

Theoretical background

Interaction

Once we talk about interaction, potential biases unfold. When initiating an online or in-person interaction, it is useful to remember the idea credited to Luísa Guimarães e Melo: '*When two people are together, they are not two but six: what each one is, what each one thinks he or she is, and what each one thinks the other is*' (Spowart, 2017, no page). Our own bias blind spots combined with our implicit and explicit biases towards others can easily influence our interactions in teaching or supervision situations. Observations of HE teacher behaviour continue to reveal differential non-verbal and academic interactions between teachers and students. We would argue that adapting our interactions to meet the needs of different learners is characteristic of effective, inclusive practice. However, as Inan-Kaya and Rubie-Davies (2021) conclude when school teachers are unaware of biases in their interactions with pupils, '[t]eacher differentiation in the treatment of students could further exacerbate the inequalities in educational outcomes that are already present in the educational system' (2021, p 11).

HEIs that embrace the pedagogy associated with deep learning endorse teacher–student and student–student interaction and students' active participation (Marton and Säljö, 1997). Deep learning is associated with more challenging taxonomic levels: application, analysis, evaluation (Anderson et al, 2001; Biggs and Collis, 1982), setting an expectation for studious, critical and informed interaction in class and during study time. However, students and teachers can find such expectations of participation and interaction challenging, and we know students can come to university with traditional conceptions of transmission teaching and passive learning (Otting et al, 2010).

This tendency for western HEIs to uphold active participation can lead to some international students being stereotyped as deficit learners, unversed in local pedagogic practices (Killick and Foster, 2021). A Chinese student at an HEI in the UK offers an alternative perception of in-class interaction: 'Here [in the UK], students achieve a good academic performance because they like to raise questions; while in China, students like to raise questions because they have a good performance' (Zhu and Gao, 2012, p 11). Gourlay cautions how 'solitary [learning] practices may be pathologised' due to the focus on student engagement (2015, p 410). Despite visiting Chinese students' efforts to adapt to western pedagogic norms, the deficit stereotype risks remaining endemic unless addressed at institutional and individual levels (Jæger and Gram, 2015; Zhu and Gao, 2012).

Group work is often planned by teachers to stimulate student–student interaction. One challenge with group work is that individual attainment can be a greater motivator than collaboration (Slavin, 2014). Therefore, in student group work situations the teacher may look for ways to delegate the tasks and responsibilities among group members, reducing interaction to organisational discourse. While task delegation can be time-efficient, it limits interaction, negotiation and cognitive elaboration. The design of group work tasks can, however, determine group member interaction and collaboration. Example 2.1 shows how the complexity and interdisciplinarity associated with solving complex tasks requires group member interaction.

Example 2.1

Making collaboration integral to the task

When a team or group has a complex interdisciplinary task to tackle, and all team members feel unsure about the process and the outcome, collaboration becomes necessary. This problem-solving approach is integrated in an engineering department's undergraduate course 'Expert in Team Innovation' (EIT). EIT is a compulsory course for most fifth-semester engineering students (approximately 400 students), who are allocated to 14 different themes. Each theme has to address a realistic complex problem that is either entrepreneurial or provided by a company. Teams within the 14 themes include students from diverse engineering programmes, nationalities and genders. The teams are facilitated by teachers from the faculty, and resources on innovation, collaboration, reflective practice and teamwork dynamics are available online. The teams are working towards team and individual course assessments.

Example 2.2

Diversity profile

During the EIT course, the students have access to resources including the diversity profile, which helps develop their collaborative learning competencies through their awareness of diversity in their groups.

Step 1 – Individual activity: Complete your own diversity profile; you will share your profile with your team in step 2. Of course, you can choose which information to share but your openness as a team is likely to help you collaborate more effectively. Reflect on your profile. How would you summarise your diversity profile? What do you think is most important to share with your team? Print out a copy of your profile, keep it anonymous.

Step 2 – Team activity: Put your profiles face down on the table and shuffle them around; each choose one and read it. When you have all read a profile, choose some information that surprised you and share it with the rest of the team; see if they can guess who you are describing. After this initial ice breaker, share and discuss your profiles more fully. Ask questions, find out what might influence how you work as a team.

> Step 3 – Team activity: Compile a list or draw a diagram representing your team's cultural experiences, competencies and approaches to teaching and learning and team-learning. What do you have in common and what are your differences? Remember both can be strengths in teams. Save a copy of this diagram/list and save your profiles; you may want to review them later in the course.

In the following section, we identify the types of bias unearthed in the dialogue. The dialogue itself then follows.

Types of bias

Law of the instrument

This cognitive bias involves a reliance on a particular tool or instrument to complete a task or solve a problem. For example, the use of rubrics and exemplification to illustrate 'what is good' is seen in academic circles as effective practice. But if the criteria are 'fuzzy' because the meaning is ambiguous, or if the students don't understand the language of the rubric or how to use it, or how to apply the exemplified material in a new context, this approach is likely to be ineffective. The student will remain unclear because the lecturer's meaning is obscure or because the student is unclear about putting the material provided into useful practice. Even where the construction of the tool is regularly reviewed, the tool itself may not work: after all, a hammer is still a hammer regardless of its size or the materials with which it is constructed.

Explicit stereotyping

Explicit stereotyping occurs where someone consciously attaches characteristics to a member of a particular group.

Bias blind spot

Each of us sees the world in a certain way, and we think of this particular way as 'reality'. Others behave differently to us, because their perception of the world is different, or rather because their perception of the world is wrong (because it is different from what we think of as 'reality'). We might attribute these different behaviours to personal characteristics or weaknesses, or we might decide that others are biased. Pronin et al (2004) argue that this way of thinking underpins the idea that not only do others hold certain biases, but that we have a tendency to deny that we hold similar biases. This is bias blind spot.

The IKEA effect

Making something yourself can have a lot of advantages. The thing that you have produced may be a better, more bespoke fit; it may be more to your individual taste; its uniqueness may appeal; you may have actually enjoyed the process of production. But what researchers found was that '*consumers also place a higher value on products they constructed themselves compared to identical items they did not construct ... [and] continue to value their own, poorly crafted creations over those which have been well crafted by an expert*' (Marsh et al, 2018, p 245). This is the IKEA effect, named after the Swedish company known particularly for flat-packed furniture designed for customers' self-assembly. It has been applied to a number of contexts, including motivating children to each more green vegetables by getting them involved in making their own meals.

Confirmation bias

Students arrive in HE with knowledge, understanding, skills, values, behaviours and experience. No two students are the same. Academics structure programmes in a manner that will enable students to access the programme content and progress. At least, this is what academics intend. Ulriksen (2009) argues that HEI course teams can presuppose a student 'type' – the '*implied student*' – which is akin to an example of confirmation bias. The notion of the '*implied student*' suggests that academics expect students to enter HE knowing what behaviours and attitudes are expected of them. Example 2.2 provides an example of an introductory team activity designed to facilitate openness and foster a trusting team culture.

In the following section, we present the dialogue, preceded by some contextual information. The dialogue is italicised, with our reflections interspersed between sections of dialogue. While the subject of the dialogue is not explicitly 'bias', the purpose of the dialogue was to unearth practice and thinking that might be associated with bias.

Using dialogue to identify bias in interaction

The dialogue: context and structure

The participants were Daniel, who asked the questions, and Jonas, who responded. The dialogue took place via Zoom and focused on an approach to the delivery of an engineering module. The participants had not met before. Daniel has substantial experience in HE; Jonas less so. Daniel knew that Jonas had adapted his approach to module delivery and had a broad sense of what this change involved and of its purpose. Daniel touched upon this in an informal exchange at the start of the dialogue, and noted that the intention was to use the GROW model as a structure for the dialogue. However, once underway, the dialogue naturally moved through the GROW steps, as Jonas's response to the *goal* question naturally flowed into an account that addressed *reality*, *options* and *will do.* This was possibly inevitable because the dialogue was about an action that Jonas had already taken and was continuing to adapt on a seminar-by-seminar basis. The alternative questions explore Jonas's evaluation of the effectiveness of the changes ('Does it work?'), probe the concept of fairness ('How did you make it fairer?') and, after Daniel talks about concerns about his own practice, the dialogue ends with some unanticipated reflections on bias.

Unpacking the dialogue

Daniel: *What was it that you wanted to achieve when adapting your approach to interactions between students?*

> Goal question

Jonas: *What I identified as a problem was while students are presenting their work – normally several presentations in a row – students are more concerned about their own presentation than learning from others' presentations. This is not productive.*

> Jonas's response takes the dialogue in a new direction, making the other GROW questions redundant

It is possible that bias blind spot underpins students' investment in their own work: they believe that their own work will be free of the prejudices and misunderstandings that they will find in other students' work. It is possible that this is an instance of the IKEA effect: the students believe their own work will be of higher value than other students' presentations. On the other hand, it could be simply that students are most focused on their own presentations rather than those of other students because of the link to assessment and grades. Jonas continues with this final line of reasoning.

Jonas: *The only one paying full attention is the teacher or facilitator, because she is evaluating the presentation. That is the problem. I needed to find a way to give the students incentive to pay attention – to maximise the learning, they all need to reflect on the work others are presenting. The incentive for 99% of students is the grade. So instead of grading their presentations, I graded the questions students give to the presenter, identifying gaps, evaluating the methodology, comparing with their own project. I tell them explicitly, 'I don't care about your presentation: I just care about how you reflect'. So the students are relaxed about their own presentation – I don't think it's fair to put pressure*

15

on both sides. I inverted the way I grade. Students are not anxious before their own presentation. They pay full attention because they need to analyse, they need to criticise, they need to compare. Usually, I encourage them to use the verbs from Bloom's taxonomy. If the students just list points, the grade is lower; if they create hypotheses, or scenarios, the grade is higher.

Evaluation
question

Daniel: *Does it work?*

Jonas: *It works pretty well. It doesn't work individually – because there is not enough time for every individual student to create their own hypothesis. I would spend the whole semester doing this. What I normally do is when one group is presenting, I put the other students in talking groups, spend time talking about their critique, their feedback. I don't like to call it 'feedback' because I received feedback from students that feedback should not receive feedback – so I call it 'critique': then I can give feedback on the critique.*

Daniel: *Semantics?*

Jonas: *Yes – semantics.*

Although Daniel is here ready to dismiss the language shift as semantic – the question implies '*Just* semantics?' – it is perhaps likely that by using an alternative term, Jonas has found a way to avoid triggering a particular interpretation of 'feedback'. Feedback is Jonas's responsibility rather than the students, and so perhaps feedback carries more risk for the students. By giving feedback they are doing Jonas's job, and this could have an unintended impact on their fellow students. It is also possible here that Daniel's interpretation, and the manner in which this interpretation is framed, closes down the discussion about language choice.

Evaluation
question

Daniel: *The problem which you identified, which was that students weren't listening to each other – in terms of addressing that problem, this has been successful. What about impact on students across the cohort? Is this a model that works consistently?*

Jonas: *I don't know if it works in mathematics or medicine. It's quite hard to create hypotheses and analyse these with chemistry or mathematics or physics, because you need to rationalise more. When you need to apply something to a context, it's easier to create a narrative and reflect on this – in my course, it's context-based.*

16

Daniel: *In terms of your subject area, this approach increases engagement between students. Does this impact more positively on some students – and less well on others?*

Jonas: *I think it worked pretty well with all students. To start, I tried grading only questions. This wasn't fair, because the first question is much easier to create than the last question. If you need to create a good question after 10 to 15 good questions, it gets harder to think critically, or differently. I tried only grading the engagement in the discussion ... but I realised that this wasn't only about engagement – they weren't thinking about analysing the overall concept: students were only thinking about creating a conversation.*

> Evaluation question leading to the concept of 'fairness'

In the critical issues feature below, we further explore the challenge identified by Jonas here.

Critical issues

Expectations of contributions from all participants

You have a class of 28 students divided into seven groups of four students. You have ensured that as far as possible the groups are 'balanced', similarly diverse, similarly confident and so forth. You present the class with a problematic scenario and ask the students to work within their groups to devise a solution. You give the students ten minutes and make it clear that each group will be given a minute to present their solution after the allotted time. Ten minutes pass. The first two groups present their solutions and you are impressed: *'Group 1, that was excellent – you've demonstrated a high level of critical thinking ... Group 2, you've found a different perspective – well done'*. Then you get to Groups 3 to 7. They have nothing to add: *'We were going to suggest the same thing as Group 1'*. Reflecting at the end of the lesson, you realise that you cannot think of anything else that the students could have reasonably suggested as solutions to the problematic scenario. The first two groups chosen to respond were always likely to come up with the most appropriate and most critical responses.

→

> One approach to address this would be to 'snowball' group ideas. Each group would note key points on a sheet (or online whiteboard) then pass the sheet onto another group for the second group's annotations. The sheets would rotate between groups, giving different groups the opportunity to add thoughts or evaluate ideas.

Later, the dialogue between Daniel and Jonas turns to the impact on student outcomes.

Daniel: *Are the students who used to be really good still the ones who are really good?*

Jonas: *What I wanted to do was create a system in which everyone is incentivised to be a good thinker: a critical thinker.*

> Probing question ⟩

Daniel: *The good ones are 'the good ones' because of their critical thinking?*

Jonas: *I say 'the good ones' not because of their grades. The good ones are the ones that think critically more often. This is what I am aiming at as an educator: critical thinking. Success in this case can mean different things for different educators. For me, it is critical thinking: think in the context, identify the gaps, find solutions, and – mostly – apply things that work in a given context, not only works generally. Perhaps for medicine or mathematics it is different: you don't need context for one plus one. In my case, you need context.*

> Daniel talks about his own concerns ⟩

Daniel: *You want your learners to be critical thinkers. It's an aim of higher education: to make students into critical thinkers. I use a lot of scaffolding: this is what this could look like. I wonder if I'm helping students to become critical thinkers, or I'm simply giving them a frame to align with.*

Jonas: *I have worked with business students before – not social science but they have a more 'social science' background. Now I'm working with engineers: they are 'in the box'. Anything that we bring from outside from like a more philosophical angle, like creating a thesis, antithesis and summary, they haven't come across this before. If I'm asking them to make a point, a counter-point and summarise everything, I call this 'being a critical thinker' – I'm not talking about critical thinking in a philosophical way. I agree with you that this shows some bias, creating a way of thinking, a particular way of thinking.*

Daniel and Jonas appear to share similar thoughts of the implied student. Both anticipate that students on their respective courses will *not be critical thinkers* when they enrol. They set out what they feel they need to do, Daniel in broad strokes (*'I use a lot of scaffolding'*) and Jonas in more detail (*'a point, a counter-point and summarise everything'*). Daniel's comment indicates implicit stereotyping (*'students enrolling in his course are not critical thinkers'*). Jonas consciously attaches a characteristic (being *'in the box'*) to engineering students as a group. In essence, this is explicit stereotyping. On the other hand, in considering these characteristics in this way, neither Daniel nor Jonas is attaching the assumed characteristic to a lack of intelligence or to something innate to the students, but are associating it with a lack of experience or prior teaching. In stereotyping the incoming students in these terms, Daniel and Jonas can plan to embed input to address this lack of experience. Through dialogue with the students and the application of formative assessment opportunities, Daniel and Jonas can explore whether the embedded input was useful.

Daniel: *To be honest, I hadn't really thought in terms of what I'm doing as a bias. But you're right: I'm creating a particular model for critical thinking which I want students to become aligned with. What I worry about is limiting their capacity for critical thinking. And you make the point that critical thinking is context-dependent: critical thinking for a social scientist and for an engineer looks very different.*

Jonas: *I think my model may not be needed in a different context. If someone is doing a programming course, if this then that, then enter the code; the world is straightforward, they don't need to see the shades of grey.*

> Jonas's response leads to an unanticipated interpretation of bias

Jonas has assumed that in a course such as one focused on programming, where the context appears to be more straightforward and less nuanced, the kind of critical thinking that Jonas is keen to encourage would be unnecessary. However, there are numerous examples of computer programming leading to biased outcomes. In 2015, for example, Amazon found that the programme devised to identify the strongest candidates from resumes submitted to the company preferred male candidates (Dastin, 2018). Gupta et al (2021) conclude that more work is needed to resolve the issue of bias in Artificial Intelligence-based candidate selection. Perhaps the kind of critical questioning that is developed in the social sciences needs to be characteristic of all degrees.

In response to the bias-related issues identified through this dialogue, we offer six strategies that teachers can employ to address bias in interactions.

Strategies to address biases in interactions

'What do you mean? I don't understand'

When students feel safe with a classroom culture, they are more likely to take risks with their learning. Students tend to feel safe when they trust their peers and teacher will interact respectfully and constructively. At the start of a course, the teacher can send a clear signal about developing a safe learning environment. They can invite students to discuss what helps them feel safe and more willing to interact and then compile and share these contributions as expectations of class/course conduct. The teacher and students can draw on their course conduct guidance, much like group rules, to remind everyone of the expected behaviour and to challenge inappropriate behaviour if it occurs.

'I don't want to ask simple questions in case everyone thinks I'm stupid'

Even when there's a safe culture, students can still be reluctant to ask basic questions in case their peers and the teacher will stereotype them as 'stupid'. This reluctance may be explained by having a fixed mindset (Dweck, 2006), which limits our will-ingness to take risks and expose our weaknesses. As students are often unaware of models which help explain learner behaviour, by introducing them to, for example, 'mastery' (Bandura, 1977) and 'fixed and open mindset' (Dweck, 2006), the teacher can reassure students and encourage them to reflect on how they could adopt a more open mindset approach towards their own and their peers' contributions.

'I prefer to work with my friends, other students' English isn't so good'

Using the standard of global English as an excuse to exclude students from groups may be indicative of stereotyping and expectation bias. In classes with linguistic diversity, having clear expectations of inclusive communication and modelling supportive inter-action are particularly relevant. The *Global People Competency Framework* (Spencer-Oatey and Stadler, 2009) includes specific guidance on intercultural communication and interpersonal competencies, with examples from UK-Sino project collaborations and in Example 2.3 we outline an online self-study resource for teachers interacting through global English.

Example 2.3

Developing inclusive international courses

Educational Quality at Universities for Inclusive International Programmes (EQUiiP, https://equiip.eu/) provides free online resources to support teachers' professional development when developing and working on inclusive international courses. The EQUiiP module on the role of language in the international classroom (EQUiiP, 2019) provides an engaging suite of activities for teacher teams on supporting linguistic diversity. EQUiiP's other modules on the international classroom complement the language module, offering a thorough and well-resourced professional development toolbox.

'I can see some students don't interact much during group work'

When teachers oversee group work activities, they may notice different levels of interaction between group members. They may assume a connection between talk and engagement, and quietness and a lack of engagement (Akinbode, 2015). If there is an expectation of student participation in group work activities, the teacher could adopt a facilitator role, schedule times to observe groups, use a sociogram to record and feedback their observations, as explained in Example 2.4.

Example 2.4

Using diagrams to represent group interactions

Sociograms (Moreno, 1934) drawn by an observer provide a diagrammatic representation of interactions within a group. Using arrows to represent forms of interaction such as inclusive questioning, replying, introducing a new point, changing the subject or criticising can help identify group member behaviour as *stars* (the most popular group members), *isolates* (those who are left out or opt out of interaction) and *cliques* (pairs or subsets with strong intra-communication, which can exclude or feel excluding to other group members). When facilitating group work, by capturing observations of group interaction with a sociogram, the facilitator can easily share their

$\longrightarrow$

observations with the group. The diagrammatic representation of the group interactions provides a useful reflection and record of individual behaviours and interactions at a specific time. Group members can be encouraged to discuss and reflect on sociograms of their interaction and to identify how patterns of interactive behaviour may affect their collaboration and their interpersonal perceptions.

Group members can then be tasked with discussing how they are including all members and ways to be more inclusive. Allocating roles to group members or using tools like the 'Six Thinking Hats' (de Bono, 1985) provide scaffolds for participatory group work and avoid group members opting out or feeling left out.

'When I meet someone new, I pause and try flipping my perceptions'

Pausing is a powerful tool; it allows us to acknowledge our initial and often unconscious '*System One*' reactions and to bring our '*System Two*' or cognitive thinking into play (Kahneman, 2011). By pausing and asking ourselves, 'if this person looked more like ...', or 'if this person sounded like ...' or 'if this person behaved like ...' would I have a different reaction? By practising the pause and flipping perceptions technique, we become more aware of how our conscious and unconscious biases influence our judgements, anchor our biases and create expectations that can be hard to overcome, and we create the opportunity to interact more thoughtfully.

Universal Design for Learning

Martin et al (2019, p 3) succinctly define Universal Design for Learning (UDL) as '*an approach based on planning for a diverse university community, rather than being surprised by diversity and attempting to retrofit adjustments for people who do not conform to the mythical norm stereotype*'. In terms of promoting interactions, providing all students with opportunities to ask questions and evaluate approaches anonymously may encourage those students who are less confident or who are uncomfortable making points or raising questions about a particular theme. Higbee (2017) suggests using weekly anonymised question cards with prompts relating to course design. There's also the 'Equality, Diversity and Inclusion' cards, which support discussion about difficult topics (University of Hertfordshire, nd). Technology, such as the noticeboard *Padlet* (www.padlet.com), provides a flexible online option for hosting students' anonymised questions. Student response systems, such as *Poll Everywhere* (www.polleverywhere.com) and *TurningPoint* (www.turning.com/pointsolutions), can be used to encourage student interactivity.

Critical questions for practice

» How do you manage your own biases when interacting with students?

» How do you encourage students to be aware of how bias may affect their own behaviour and interactions?

» How would you relate examples and insights from this chapter to your experiences with online interactions?

Summary

- Bias is present in interactions but there are opportunities to act constructively and to recognise and scaffold students' strengths and areas for development.

- Critical dialogues provide opportunities for both the coachee and the coach to unearth their own biases.

- Critical dialogues can provide opportunities to unpick practice and identify transferable features.

- Teachers' stereotypes of students can trigger positive action if teachers respond critically to these conscious biases.

- While the model of the successful student is one who is engaged and participating, be mindful of students' diverse approaches to learning.

Useful texts

Gourlay, Lesley (2015) 'Student Engagement' and the Tyranny of Participation, *Teaching in Higher Education*, 20(4): 402–11.

Gourlay challenges the traditional models of what student participation looks like and recognises that student participation is continually evolving.

Inan-Kaya, Gamze and **Rubie-Davies**, Christine (2021) Teacher Classroom Interactions and Behaviours: Indications of Bias. *Learning and Instruction*. [online] Available at: https://doi.org/10.1016/j.learninstruc.2021.101516 (accessed 12 January 2022).

Inan-Kaya and Rubie-Davies's research explores how teachers' biases are manifested in their classroom interactions with learners.

Ulriksen, Lars (2009) The Implied Student. *Studies in Higher Education*, 34(5): 517–32.

Ulriksen uses the concept of 'the implied student' not as the basis of a toolbox to address bias or inequality, but as an approach to support our thinking about student experience in higher education.

Course design and content

Introduction

Biases influence course design. Chapter 3 explores how course designers can mitigate the impact of bias. When course designers are aware of biases, they employ structure and content in ways to build inclusive and universally accessible courses. All courses have external and internal parameters. External parameters include national curricular requirements, professional standards and politico-social norms (to which the dialogue in this chapter refers). Institutional parameters include validation requirements and the associated practical framework defined by the number of credits or study hours assigned to the course. Within a course such as an undergraduate degree, parameters are set at different levels of leadership: for example, the course leadership prefers to maintain an approach to course design that maintains the status quo (see below for an explanation of the status quo bias). The course designer's diversity of knowledge and openness to new thinking represent further parameters. Where the course designer has the capacity to innovate, this will be compromised by explicit or implicit expectations about maintaining the status quo. Through unpicking the coaching dialogue in this chapter, we explore the impact on course design of two specific biases: status quo bias and authority bias.

Theoretical background

When planning HE course curricular content and pedagogical design, we need to be mindful of biases. Biases of particular significance in this context are status quo bias, where we, where we conform to norms, and authority bias, where we can be influenced by those in authority positions, even if their knowledge is not authoritative. HE course design is rarely an independent process. Alongside whatever preferences course designers may bring, external requirements impose their own criteria and biases on course design. These external parameters include, for example, national curricula (Department for Education, 2014), those issued by professional bodies (such as the Quality Assurance Agency, nd), HEIs' strategies, budget and resource limitations, and societal and other stakeholder expectations.

Looking at an example of externally imposed curricular parameters, such as the national curriculum for school education in England (Department for Education, 2014), we see how it imposes a culturally limited perspective of UK history

(Mansfield, 2019) and how it devalues the creative curriculum (The Warwick Commission, 2015). While HE may not be directly bound by national curricula designed for school education, HE students and lecturers are likely to be encultured by social norms and curricular interpretations. To enable course designers to effectively challenge epistemic neutrality and to make the social and cultural histories of their academic subjects explicit (Azumah Dennis, 2018; Gandolfi, 2021), course designers can access HE case studies designed to close the UK attainment gap for Black, Asian and minority ethnic (BAME) students (Amos and Doku, 2019b) and decolonised reading lists (Prescod-Weinstein, 2015; University of Westminster, nd). Two examples of resources designed to support decolonising course curricula, University College London's *Inclusive Curriculum Health Check* and the University of Huddersfield's *Reading List Toolkit,* are described in Example 3.1.

Example 3.1

Resources supporting decolonising the curriculum

The *Inclusive Curriculum Health Check* (University College London, nd) provides a list of questions designed to stimulate discussion and action by course designers, teachers and leaders to check the level of inclusion designed for and experienced by HE students. The checklist includes sub-lists for curriculum, teaching and learning, and assessment.

The *Reading List Toolkit* (University of Huddersfield, nd) provides a portal to a variety of non-western university libraries, links to decolonised reading lists prepared by UK universities and links to additional resources developed by BAME HE staff and students. To help compile a reading list with diverse author representation, the Toolkit suggests using Social Media and Google Scholar or Scopus to access profiles of researchers at non-Western HE institutions (HEIs) and/or those with BAME heritage.

Shifting our focus to internal parameters, designing a course with clear alignment between learning objectives, assessment and learning activities can signal transparency and fairness. Biggs (1996) calls this constructive alignment. There are different course design models which support inclusive course design which is '*meaningful, relevant and accessible to all*' (Hockings, 2010, p 1). With some students, the potential barriers to learning will be visible or at least more obvious, and course designers can address these by removing the barriers that university course designers may traditionally erect. However, for other students the barriers may be less obvious and as a consequence, courses may be less inclusive. An approach to course design that adopts the principles of UDL (see Chapter 2, page 22) would present course content to all students in diverse ways and would provide all students with multiple ways through which to engage with that content (Merry, 2021), thereby accommodating all students' strengths and needs, whether these were visible or not. When applying Killick's (2015b) *Aspire, Design and Evaluate* course design model, the design process starts with identifying the values, objectives and capabilities the course will address. By adopting approaches such as these, course designers signal inclusion and bias mitigation from the outset. This inclusivity can be developed further through the adoption of an internationalised curriculum, which attributes value to diversity and heralds a globally inclusive course (Killick and Foster, 2021). And when course design involves a wider partnership, including for example students and employers in collaboration and co-creation, this can release alternative perspectives and insights that facilitate students' development of competencies necessary for '*the globalising world of their futures*' (Killick, 2015b, p 4).

Types of bias

Status quo educational bias

MacMullen (2011, p 873) explores the idea of status quo bias in civic education. He defines status quo bias as: '*behavior by adults (including but not limited to educators acting in their professional capacity) whose (sometimes unintended) effect is to encourage children's belief in the substantive merits of a particular existing law or political institution*'. Status quo educational bias is not biased towards alternative political forms. MacMullen argues that by promoting awareness of status quo educational bias, educators may more effectively identify approaches to enable learners to make informed choices as citizens.

Authority bias

We live with and in hierarchical systems, which rely on some having greater authority than others. Some have authority because we have granted this: for example, we elect politicians and, in general, rely on those elected to make appropriate decisions for the region or country as a whole. Some have authority because others with greater authority have granted this: for example, some of us have line managers and some of us will line manage others. Some have authority because of certificated expertise: doctors, for example, study and develop their practice over many years. The word 'authority' carries two similar but distinct meanings: a position of authority, placing one person over another in a hierarchy, allowing the person in authority to demand acquiescence; or authority in the sense of knowledge or experience which might lead us to look to someone who is an authority for advice or guidance – a medical doctor or a captain piloting an aeroplane. Authority bias describes a tendency to accept the view of someone in a position of authority, regardless of whether or not they are an authority on the issue they express views about.

Critical issues

Addressing authority bias

How might authority bias affect course designers' judgements over curricula, references and pedagogy? Gladwell (2008) provides an example of authority bias in action, although he does not label it as such. Gladwell looks at similarities between circumstances leading to aeroplane crashes. He concludes that crashes are significantly more likely when the captain, that is, the most senior person in the cockpit, is flying the plane. Gladwell argues this is because if the captain were in the role of second pilot, the captain would not hesitate to bluntly point out the first pilot's error. However, when the captain is the first pilot, the second pilot might be less direct. People who are less senior in the hierarchy tend to *mitigate* their language. In other words, they '*downplay or sugarcoat the meaning of what is being said*' (Gladwell, 2008, p 194) when speaking to someone in authority. What if we applied Gladwell's example to a course design team, which includes colleagues with different institutional roles and status, together with students recruited as partners or co-contributors? How could the team ensure inclusion, so that all involved are enabled to have a voice, and that all contributions are valued during the design process?

In the following section we provide some contextual information about the dialogue and then present the dialogue itself. The dialogue is punctuated by our reflections relating to the biases identified above.

Using dialogue to identify bias in course design

The dialogue: context and structure

Rob, who has a background in teaching in compulsory and post-compulsory education, asks the questions. Mary, whose background is in research, responds. However, as the dialogue proceeds, it is worth noting that they begin to collaboratively construct ways of describing the challenges and of identifying solutions. The dialogue starts with the *Reality* question. Then, rather than identify a *Goal*, Rob asks Mary about the challenges of designing a module such as the one they are discussing. The dialogue then moves onto *Options*, when Rob asks Mary how she overcomes the challenges identified. However, this question effectively unearths further layers of challenge. Rob does not ask Mary to commit to action but rather answers the unspoken question on Mary's behalf, stating: *'You're very committed to the idea of sort of challenging these limited and limiting perspectives'.*

Unpacking the dialogue

Rob: *Can you just tell me a bit about the context of the module that you're going to be thinking about?*

> Reality question

Mary: *We're talking about a module which explores international perspectives of education. It's a compulsory third-year module ... And I guess it builds on what we've done in previous modules, so looking at ideas around curriculum, policy, pedagogy: things that we introduced quite a lot in the first year. Hopefully it builds on that. And it sits alongside another third-year module which explores challenging or controversial issues in education, so the module we're discussing may contribute to students' understanding of or thinking about challenging issues. And it helps a few of them think about their dissertation project title: some students end up doing something like 'decolonising history'. One student did that last year and they said that was sort of inspired by this module. But yeah, one of my hopes is that it just helps their thinking about all aspects of education, not necessarily just international issues.*

Rob: *But the focus of this module involves thinking about education in an international way?*

Mary: *Yes, thinking about education in a global context. One of the ways I kind of see it is that by seeing that things happen differently in different places, it helps you to recognise the things that seem inevitable are not inevitable: they could be otherwise because they are otherwise in other places. But what's maybe a bit complex is that that sits alongside the fact that we're looking very much at globalisation and have particular ideas of how education travelled around the world. And you do see incredible similarities around the world. So the idea that it's possible to be different is partly undermined.*

Mary is interested in addressing status quo education bias. She argues that by looking at a subject from an unfamiliar angle, the module might trigger students' awareness of alternative possibilities.

Rob: *That's really very clear. Thinking about the content of the module and maybe the delivery of the module, what types of challenge do you face in the context of this module? What makes it difficult? What do you have to overcome?*

Mary: *So ... the world is huge. I know quite a lot about education policy in England. When I'm presenting to them, OK, let's try and get some understanding of how education policy operates in a particular country, let's say Finland. Then I talk to them about the limitations of what they can know about what education is like in Finland and the fact that it's really hard to find out just from a distance what education is actually like, and there are different ways. I quite often give students the example of if someone from the other side of the world was to come and look at English policy documents, they might look at the national curriculum and be like, 'OK, so this is what children in England are learning'. Whereas actually they would be way off any true sense of what children in England are learning: the children may never have got any citizenship education, for example. What they actually learn is very much shaped by the testing regime so children spend much more time on some subjects at the cost of other subjects and then I would also need to look at the contextual information: for example, you've got academies which don't have to follow the national curriculum anyway. Let's say, if you were investigating what happens in English schools, you might think: OK, I'm going to look at the national curriculum, but that wouldn't tell you what was actually happening in classrooms in England. I try to teach students about that as a sort of methodological problem. That's one side of it. But on the other side I have this problem: I'm trying to teach the students about the education system in Finland but I don't really know as much as I should about the education system in Finland myself, because I'm facing all those issues that I'm presenting to them as issues. Similar problem to the last problem, right? I tell them about the contradictions, but the contradictions still exist.*

Mary implies that challenging status quo educational bias is difficult in part because our own knowledge of alternative approaches is limited, and limiting. It may be that our status as academics is rooted in our expertise about a subject in a particular context.

Mary also acknowledges that she is *not* an authority on everything she talks about *with authority*. For example, she feels that she does not know as much about the Finnish education system as she should. She recognises that students are unlikely to question the extent of her knowledge: in essence, the students are subject to authority bias. However, she is aware of this possibility, and continues to pursue this theme in her subsequent response.

Rob: *So how could you overcome this?*

> Options question

Mary: *I guess from the point of view of students' learning, kind of getting to focus on a couple of countries, rather than making sweeping generalisations: that's for them. Then for me, getting that sort of range of knowledge about a place, like I mentioned Finland, I might talk quite a bit about Chile just because I've been there and I know people there. I've got a bit of an understanding. There's something about me focusing, I guess, as well. But then, students need to focus, but it's always going to be inadequate. Students need to sort of recognise how inadequate that is.*

Rob: *You're very committed to the idea of challenging these limited and limiting perspectives, and we could apply this more generally across other subjects. I know we're talking specifically here about the field of education, but actually, you could question the approach to teaching* Science, Technology, Engineering and Maths (STEM) *subjects in a similar way, look at the kind of limited, limiting perspective: recognising that this is how we do it here and thinking beyond that. Have you used any approaches with students that have been particularly successful? Have there been any kind of breakthroughs, eureka moments?*

> Rob draws his own conclusions and attempts to broaden the focus of the dialogue

Rob attempts to apply Mary's thinking about challenging students' thinking in the specific context of educational policy and practice more generally. He proposes that there is a universal notion that academics and students of any subject may be limited in their thinking by the context in which they live and work. Is the thinking of students of STEM subjects, for example, limited by familiar or embedded behaviours? Researchers writing about STEM subject teaching imply that this limited thinking is present and offer solutions. For example, Resnick and Rosenbaum (2013, p 164), exploring possibilities in STEM subject teaching, propose *tinkering* as a solution, characterising it as '*a playful, experimental, iterative style of engagement, in which makers are continually reassessing their goals, exploring new paths, and imagining new possibilities*'. Poce et al (2019, p 103) argue that tinkering represents '*a meaningful method not only to develop scientific knowledge, but also to promote 21st century skills*'. This notion of twenty-first century skills chimes neatly with the transformative competencies identified by the Organisation for Economic Co-operation and Development (OECD, 2019, p 2), in particular the idea that students should be enabled to recognise and take account of '*the many interconnections and inter-relations between seemingly contradictory or incompatible ideas*'.

The dialogue continues.

Mary: *Often I think it is about understanding the minutiae of something. Because it's so hard to know which things could be different. So, for example, I was talking with the students about neoliberalism as being such a dominant discourse that we're not conscious of it and we're not aware of it necessarily. We are living in the neoliberal world but we don't recognise it. It's like being a fish swimming in the sea not recognising that it's living in water. And how in the first year, when I first introduced the idea of neoliberalism, I talk about communism, which they all say that they've heard of: they recognise communism as an ideology that shapes the way things operate because it's outside of them, it's a different time and place. Whereas neoliberalism, they find incredibly hard to see – as we all do – because we're living in it. From the point of view of what we could do about that, apart from just saying really useless things like 'question everything', I guess, for a lot of subjects, maybe there is an assumption that a lot of things are universals which are not necessarily universals ... But, questioning those sorts of very, very deep assumptions like: 'Well, of course, the best way to know how good a school is to measure and test the kids and compare scores, I mean, that's obvious, how else could you possibly do it?' It's so kind of common-sense-obvious to us. It's really hard for people to say, 'But hang on, perhaps that's not the best way of measuring how good a school is'. I think that's maybe one of my issues, maybe with some of the recent decolonising literature: it's on that very clearly abstract level, which inevitably it has to be at first. But then you have to get into the real deep specifics like, for example, I don't know, focus on brick manufacturing and then find out about all sorts of different perspectives on brick manufacturing in order to recognise that what you thought is universal is actually very ... contextual.*

Mary also implies that developing thinking to challenge status quo educational bias is difficult because all of us – students and academics – cannot necessarily see that our perspective is limited.

Mary uses analogies or images to help students challenge their functional fixedness bias (see Chapter 5) and understand abstract or complex concepts. Earlier in the dialogue, she describes how she asks students to imagine '*someone from the other side of the world*' drawing conclusions about UK practice from looking at policy documents. In the passage above, to illustrate the ubiquity of neoliberalism, Mary uses the image of a fish swimming in the sea, unaware that it is surrounded by water. Pinker (2015, p 72) argues that we often forget the significance of the visual, and '*for us to go from "I think I understand" to "I understand" we need to see the sights and feel the motions*'.

Rob: *Is it then just around developing students' critical thinking? Getting them to question?*

> Rob attempts to draw a simplistic conclusion

Mary: *Yeah, but you say 'just' as if that's ...*

Rob: *'Just'! [LAUGHS]*

Mary: *I guess that is the ultimate thing that we want to do, but ... I mean, the way people talk about critical thinking is another whole story, right? The government's always saying it wants to promote critical thinking, but it doesn't really mean critical thinking in the sense that they want people to question anything the government says, for example. There are so many different ways you might understand that. But, yeah, that kind of idea of challenging assumptions is the main thing.*

In consideration of the bias-related issues identified through this dialogue, we offer six strategies that teachers can employ to address bias in course and curricular design.

Strategies to address biases in course design and content

Checklists

Checklists help address our fallible memories, as we tend to remember highlights rather than the complete picture. When designing a course, we can draw on a variety of checklists and toolkits which support the development of an inclusive curriculum and course design. University College London's '*Inclusive Curriculum Health Check*' (introduced in Example 3.1) offers three categories: 1. Content, 2. Teaching and learning, 3. Assessment. Each category offers statements, with a traffic light system to help grade a course's inclusive qualities and identify areas in need of action. For example, in 1. Content, course designers are asked to evaluate '*to what extent does your programme curriculum – Develop students' critical thinking and awareness of different perspectives on issues relating to diversity in ethnicity, culture and nationality?'* The course designers would then evaluate whether there is evidence that the content addresses this fully, partly or if there is no evidence.

Decolonising the curriculum

University libraries are obvious places to start when seeking advice on decolonising reading lists and curricula. The library at the University of Arts, London, has produced a toolkit with four sections: 1. Engage with the library support offer, 2. Question your reading list, 3. Find the marginalised voice, 4. Co-create interventions with students. In section 2, you will find a suite of questions that would inform a course design discussion such as 'What are the dominant voices and narratives in your areas of study?' and 'What voices and narratives are excluded, and how can they be identified?'

If your library does not currently provide a comparable toolkit, mobilising teachers' and students' interest can often provide the necessary impetus; see Bhambra et al's (2018) collection of academic essays on decolonising the university for examples of institutional initiatives. We can all start by updating course reading lists to ensure they include subject research and studies by scholars committed to decolonisation and redressing colonial superiority. Prescod-Weinstein's (2015) and Kara's (2020) web resources provide relevant references for decolonising curricular content, methods and methodologies, which are directly relevant for research and project work.

Universal Design

Universal Design (UD) is also known as Universal Design for Learning (UDL) and Universal Design for Education (UDE). Burgstahler (2021, p 1) states that UD is *'proactive and benefits all students, including those who are not receiving disability-related accommodations and other services'*. UD is not a bespoke package aimed at an individual learner, but an approach that acknowledges and addresses all of the possible barriers that all students might face, enabling learners with diverse abilities and preferences to flourish. For example, UD-informed practice would ensure that *all learners* have access to course resources presented in multiple ways: printed on paper, as e-documents with embedded hyperlinks, through a podcast, subtitled video and so on.

Student consultation partnership

Involving students in and consulting students about course design is recommended by inclusive course design approaches and toolkits (University of Arts, London, nd) and advocates student partnership (Bovill, 2020). One example of a student partnership as illustrated in Example 3.2 was during the revalidation process for a suite of graduate programmes for pre-service teachers at a UK university with distributed campuses. These programmes were accessed via a blend of online resources, in-person teaching and learning, and school-based experiential placements.

Example 3.2

Student partnership during revalidation process

As course leader of a suite of graduate courses, Donna was involved with revalidation. This was a year-long process, working in collaboration with teachers and student mentors from local schools, lecturers involved with the graduate programme, former and current students, and educational developers. To signal the importance of student partnership, former and current students from the graduate programmes were invited to participate in the revalidation process as co-creators. This reciprocal creative process led to new insights about course content, online provision and face-to-face teaching. Some of the former students were working as qualified teachers, which meant they contributed both student and professional perspectives on what was needed from the next iterations of the graduate programmes. Together they updated the graduate programmes, enabling streamlined course provision and assessment – they moved from multiple short modules to three modules, updated online self-audits and self-study units for subject knowledge, implemented clear criteria for in-person teaching, and included regular focus group meetings with students and inbuilt feedback mechanisms. Without the students' collaboration, the programme leaders and teachers would have missed vital insights into student experiences and what they prioritised as busy, pragmatic learners.

A connected curriculum

In the foreword to *A Connected Curriculum for Higher Education* (Fung, 2017), Barnett invites the reader '*to a new idea of the university, a university that is fully ecological, attending carefully to the many ecosystems in its midst*' (Fung, 2017, p vii). The book explores and advocates connectivity between all aspects of programme design, reinforcing the opportunities to enrich teaching, learning and research through collaborations. Chapter 4 on 'Connected programme design' offers ten approaches including interconnected mandatory modules or courses and a combined programme assessment. Such approaches challenge course silos which encourage a tick-box approach to completing each course without understanding how courses interconnect. Instead, by integrating a capstone module the course and programme design can send a clear signal that learning across the programme's courses is relevant and meaningful as the students have to draw on their inter-course learning and apply it to a complex problem. The book's premise that *'Education is not a set of technicalities; it embodies an intellectual and ethical position'* reaffirms course designers' responsibilities and how their curricular and pedagogical choices influence those who teach and those who learn (ibid, p 15).

Interdisciplinary approaches: time to rethink

Interdisciplinary learning is nothing new: Hypatia and Leonardo da Vinci were two polymaths doing it years ago! The vertically integrated interdisciplinary project consortium, VIP, facilitates inter-university research, and teaching and learning collaborations (http://vip-consortium.org/). VIP projects offer students and researchers opportunities to co-create new interdisciplinary knowledge through team-based, experiential learning. This may be exemplary interdisciplinarity but with the current focus on addressing complex global problems and sustainability, planning and facilitating interdisciplinary HE courses is an inevitable response to complex global problems. In its *Conceptual Learning Framework*, the Organisation for Economic Co-operation and Development (OECD, 2019, p 2) advocates enabling students to develop these three interdisciplinary graduate competencies.

1. Creating new value – *because it 'blends a sense of purpose with critical thinking and creativity'.*

2. Reconciling tensions and dilemmas – because in our increasingly complex world, students need to *'become comfortable with complexity and ambiguity'.*

3. Taking responsibility – because those *'who have the capacity to take responsibility for their actions have a strong moral compass that allows for considered reflection, working with others and respecting the planet'.*

Critical questions for practice

» How can HE institutions enable decolonised curricula and inclusive pedagogies? What are the barriers and constraints and how can they be overcome?

» Status quo bias limits variation and novelty. Who has agency in the course design process to pursue different approaches and to include novelty in course design?

» When course designers invite students to co-design a course, how can they ensure student voices are valued, heard and acted upon?

Summary

- Course designers' decisions are limited by national and institutional parameters, as well as by biases embedded in the course itself and by course designers' own biases.

- Critical dialogues provide opportunities to share approaches to challenge or mitigate the impact of these parameters and biases.

- Biases such as those discussed in this chapter apply to all subject fields and are not limited to the social sciences.

- Raising students' awareness of bias is important and can be challenging.

- There is a range of easily accessible tools to support course designers in challenging bias.

Useful texts

Burgstahler, Sheryl (2021) *Universal Design in Education: Principles and Applications, Disabilities, Opportunities, Internetworking, and Technology.* [online] Available at: www.washington.edu/doit/sites/default/files/atoms/files/UDE-Principles-and-Applications.pdf (accessed 12 January 2022).

An accessible overview of Universal Design which clarifies the relationship between the roots of UD in architecture and its application to teaching and learning. The UD of Instruction (UDI) section provides some useful examples to inform course designers' thinking and teaching practice.

Fung, Dilly (2017) *A Connected Curriculum for Higher Education.* [online] Available at: https://discovery.ucl.ac.uk/id/eprint/1558776/1/A-Connected-Curriculum-for-Higher-Education.pdf (accessed 12 January 2022).

A Connected Curriculum provides clear rationales and practical insights into ways to connect the different elements and stakeholders involved with curricular or programme design. Through this integration, students and teachers are more likely to experience meaningful and relevant HE curricula.

University of Arts, London (nd) *Decolonising Reading Lists.* [online] Available at: www.arts.ac.uk/__data/assets/pdf_file/0021/201936/Decolonising-reading-lists-PDF-703KB.pdf (accessed 12 January 2022).

This is a useful and thoughtfully constructed set of steps towards taking course reading lists beyond the white, male, Western perspective which is often embedded in reading lists. Questioning the 'dominant voice' and co-creation with students are key to this process.

Introduction

In this chapter, we focus on how student responses to learning activities can be affected by biases, particularly planning fallacy bias and law of triviality bias (Benson, 2016). We suggest strategies that could be employed to mitigate the impact of these biases or even prevent them from arising in the first place. The coaching dialogue also unearths how reflecting again on past practice can reveal new understanding for the lecturer, providing opportunities to challenge what we might have come to accept as 'good practice'. In essence this is an opportunity to explore status quo bias (see Chapter 3), where the norm has been constructed by the lecturer themselves rather than imposed or set in stone by the practice of a university team or department.

Theoretical background

According to Biggs and Tang (2007), when learning activities are designed to align with a course's learning outcomes (LOs) and assessment, they can provide student learners with meaningful, experiential and challenging ways to learn. When planning learning activities, lecturers may set out to engage and challenge students with authentic learning opportunities, and encourage them to take more ownership, to be more proactive and to contribute to a more inclusive learning environment. Lecturers may require learners to negotiate a complex global issue. They may want learners to work collaboratively or to develop intercultural competencies. However, even when lecturers are committed to inclusive practices such as these, biases come into play.

We could expect HE courses to engage students with challenging learning activities, designed to provoke critical, divergent and novel thinking. However, students' perceptions of these learning activities and the associated learning processes are vulnerable to those biases which affect workers in organisations. Studies reveal how trivialising routine practices and engaging in conformist groupthink (Manz and Neck, 1995) at organisational, group and individual levels limits employees' critical and divergent thinking (Mnasri and Papakonstandinidis, 2020; Zalewski et al, 2017). Imagine groups of HE students tasked with discussing a controversial issue and summarising their thoughts on a poster: they may spend a disproportionate time discussing the design of the poster rather than the learning activity, effectively trivialising the process of unpicking the layers of the focus issue. Students and employees are similarly susceptible to the law of triviality bias, which ushers them towards the easier elements of a task rather than facing up to the time and resources needed to engage with its more complex elements.

To further compound the problem, the same student group may have been influenced by the planning fallacy bias when they misconstrued the complexity of the learning activity or overestimated their own capabilities. The planning fallacy bias leads learners to allocate insufficient time and resources to learning activities, resulting in superficial engagement with the learning process and possibly unfinished products. To further compound the problem, getting side-tracked by the law of triviality bias or falling prey to the planning fallacy bias could trigger the IKEA effect bias (see Chapter 2), where the student group believes their teacher or peers should give greater acknowledgement to their design efforts, even when unwarranted.

Group work: sameness or novelty?

Familiarity helps us feel safe, and we need to feel safe if we are going to take risks (Allport, 1954/1979; Harrison, 2012). By contrast, when group members do not know each other or are uncertain or concerned about how others perceive them, this can induce discomfort and reduce risk-taking (Kahneman, 2011). However, for all its advantages, feeling safe among familiar group members can also stifle creativity and limit opportunities for diversity. For example, when students can choose their own groups, they often prefer to conform to their in-group biases and self-select. In turn, this in-group homogeneity tends to foster conformity and group-think wherein the group members reinforce rather than challenge each other's ideas (Manz and Neck, 1995). While diversity can lead to more creativity and novel ideas than when in-group groupthink prevails (Philips et al, 2006), other enabling factors have to be in place. Just putting a mixture of people together in a team does not automatically lead to more creative and novel output. In fact, unless the team output requires collaboration and the team members are open to differences, to challenge and to novelty, biases can be reinforced and output can be compromised (Killick, 2015a). Example 4.1 describes how a video portraying a dysfunctional group provides a useful resource to help challenge viewers' conceptions of group members as in-group and outsiders.

Example 4.1

Supporting inclusive group work

The formation of cliques can challenge inclusive group work (Moreno, 1934). Three students at a Danish university volunteered to co-develop a ten-minute video resource (Centre for Teaching and Learning, 2016) about group work to highlight how easily cliques can develop within groups, leaving another isolated and misunderstood. The video's focus on factors that contribute to collaborative group work provides a useful workshop resource. In the video, no matter how the isolated student tries to validate her behaviour, the clique-pair has already categorised her as unreliable and they ignore her explanations, which results in confirming the clique/isolate dynamic. (You can read about Moreno's analysis of social links in groups in Chapter 2.)

When using the video (Centre for Teaching and Learning, 2016) in workshops on group work, participants are asked to note their initial reactions to each of the three characters, listing keywords that come to mind. These initial reactions provide examples of what Kahneman (2011) refers to as our rapid, unconscious and unprocessed '*System One*' thinking. The shared video engages the course participants in a shared experience. They are invited to share their keywords and to discuss what informed their initial reactions to the three group members' behaviours and how on reflection they might change any biased reactions.

Types of bias

The dialogue between the book's two authors, which you can read below, elicits two types of bias in particular: planning fallacy bias and the law of triviality. Donna appears to become more aware and more critical of established patterns in her practice.

Using dialogue to identify bias in interaction

The dialogue: context and structure

In this dialogue, Donna responds to Andrew's questions. Donna and Andrew have worked together for many years and they have experience co-designing and teaching the same modules at an HEI. The particular course that Donna refers to in this dialogue was a global citizenship component of a primary teacher training programme, where Donna's original intention was to develop students' curricular knowledge as well as their understanding of pedagogy. Because these are teacher training students, the students have some understanding of the idea of LOs and of the idea of learning about learning. The dialogue retains some of the spirit of the GROW model, although the participants' familiarity with each other's practice and thinking means that the dialogue develops more organically.

Unpacking the dialogue

| Goal question |

Andrew: *So, Donna, when you are planning student activities as part of a module session, what are your priorities?*

Donna: *Well, what I should say is that my priorities are to check that the learning activity is aligned with the learning outcome and the assessment. And then to make sure that the learning activity is achievable for the students in the time that I'm giving them and with the resources that are provided. And to provide clear instructions on what I expect them to both do and achieve from being involved in this learning activity. So those are the ideals, but whether I achieve those, I very much doubt I do in most situations achieve all of them. And I think one of the big challenges is making the tacit explicit. So, what I have in my mind is a clearly designed learning activity that will enable them to learn this. I'm sure that I don't always express that as clearly as I could. I can think of an example. When I was teaching a global citizenship class at a UK university, the students were in groups and each group either chose or was given a foodstuff. They had to map the origins of the foodstuff, looking at stakeholder involvement and … the journey, really, of this foodstuff, from where it started its life to it being in a local supermarket. And very deliberately, actually, my approach with this activity was different: the students weren't given the learning outcomes at the start – this is what I would usually do when I taught student teachers, I'd give them learning outcomes, because I was modelling the practice that the student teachers were expected to take into the classroom. But with this activity, I deliberately didn't share learning outcomes, because I wanted the students to deconstruct their learning from the activity and to identify what learning outcomes they had actually engaged with as part of the task.*

Example 4.2

Withholding LOs

Are LOs only precise and measurable because the teacher has an unconscious expectation of what they are looking for (Hussey and Smith, 2003)? Could withholding LOs be a way to offset the inevitability of the planning fallacy and the law of triviality? Models for teaching global citizenship encourage teachers to adopt a participatory learning environment, in which learners become increasingly active, take responsibility and collaborate. When we share LOs with learners at the start of a session, this brings certainty and, potentially, disappointment if learners do not feel they have learnt what was intended by the end of the session. It also confines the learning: '*You will learn no more than this*'. Oxfam's *Global Citizenship in the Classroom* (2015, p 5), for example, argues that learners should develop the '*ability to manage complexity and uncertainty*'. Where there is an expectation that learners deconstruct learning activities and identify their own LOs, students are less likely to see activities as tick-box exercises. And maybe the fun and expectation that can be associated with the new is kept active.

Donna continues: *And it wasn't a classroom that was equipped with Internet access and lots of computers, it was just a standard classroom. I didn't have the expectation that they would go out of class and research the question, they just had to get on with it in the 20 or so minutes they were given, and most groups did that. But now, on reflection, I know that some of the groups were equipped with more experienced members than others, and by that, I mean these were graduates who had returned to university to train to be teachers, so some of them had a lot more life experience because some of them came straight from their undergraduate course onto this postgraduate course, but many of them had worked in all sorts of different jobs before they joined the course. So, some of them had direct experience of sales, of marketing, of ... transportation. You know, they could tune into this much more easily than others. And there was one group which didn't really have anybody with this wider life experience, and they struggled to really engage with the task, and they completed it very quickly at a very, I would say, superficial level. And even when I went back and tried to check that they understood, they just didn't have the resources within the group to be able to develop the activity further. That experience stayed with me as an example of ... well, me really not having considered that there could be a group that didn't have inner resources to be able to rise to the challenge of the task. So, when at the end of the task I asked the students to deconstruct their participation in the activity, to identify the knowledge, skills and competencies which they had used to engage in the activity, this particular group's list was relatively short compared with the lists of other groups. The other groups had engaged with a lot of negotiation, argument, critiquing, careful listening, analysing responses ... But this particular group just responded with: 'Well, we don't know anything about tea. And that's it, really'. So, it made me aware of the further preparation I should have done.*

Reality question 1

Andrew: *How aware were the students in that class of this subsequent activity involving unpicking the skills, the competencies that you're going to ask them to consider?*

Donna: *Yeah, I don't think I said at the start that that's what they would have to do. I was just clear that in this activity, 'I'm deliberately not sharing the learning outcomes with you now. And let's leave it at that for now' because I wanted them just to get on and not be too conscious of what they were doing. But then I gave them time at the end of the activity to reflect on the knowledge, skills and competencies they had used when engaging in this task. And then I asked each group to share those in the plenary and we compiled them in a list.*

Reality question 2

Andrew: *Were there any other factors that contributed to the way the students responded?*

Donna: *Well, it was one group of, I guess, five or six students. There was a kind of resistance from them because the global citizenship class was a one-off, integrated into an education studies programme. So, you know, I suspect it wasn't their choice to come to a global citizenship class, it doesn't fire everybody up, doesn't feel important for everyone. And because it also wasn't and still isn't part of the school curriculum, they could very easily say, 'Well, I'm never going to teach this, I'm never going to use it, it's not useful'. So, I don't know, to be honest, what was blocking them from being more creative, but it could have been any of those factors.*

Andrew: *So, if you were to do an activity with similar aims where you're wanting students to identify for themselves the kind of meta dimensions of the learning, how would you approach it now?*

> Options question

Donna: *Well, if I were to do the same activity again, I think I would give more thought to ... not so much the deconstruction part, because I think that failed with this group, because they really hadn't employed much knowledge, skills or competencies in the task, you know, so they didn't have much to reflect on. But I would give more thought to the group composition, you know, who's actually in the group in terms of the diversity of background knowledge that they could possibly bring. Although saying that, I was really surprised by just how much individual knowledge and experience some of the other groups had. But maybe I could just forewarn the students and encourage them to make their own groups more diverse to start with.*

Example 4.3

Learners taking control of group composition

Donna describes an approach:

> *I used to do an activity for which I wanted the learners to be in diverse groups. I would briefly summarise the task, then ask the learners to share with each other the knowledge, skills, and competencies that they bring. Sometimes learners would make a simple sign saying, 'I know about this, I have skills in this, I have competencies in this'. I wanted each group to be diverse in terms of the knowledge, skills and competencies the learners brought to the group.*

This took individual students '*out of their respective comfort zones and was a way to get the learners to think collectively and critically about what the task involved*'. This approach encourages self-reflection, another key skill identified by Oxfam (2015). It also provides a way to overcome planning fallacy bias, since the diversity of the group may encourage a more questioning or critical approach when considering the challenge presented by the task.

Andrew: *You've talked about your own expectations and how you were surprised by the body of knowledge that some of the groups brought. Do you feel some students brought obstacles to the process, things which made it harder for them to make the most of the experience? I suppose I mean blockers.*

> Repetitive question

Andrew's question returns to ground that Donna has already covered and her response opens by noting this. However, in this case the repeated question triggers new thinking.

Donna: *Yeah, I guess, I mean, those I've maybe indicated you know, if they're not interested in the subject, it doesn't motivate them. And thinking about students who are going to be teachers there in the UK system, they at the time anyway were very constrained by what's in the national curriculum. So 'If it isn't [in the curriculum], I don't need to know because I don't have to teach it'. Which I think is a tragedy. But, yeah, that was an understandable parameter. But maybe what I would call the stronger groups, you know, the ones that were engaging with the task, if they had an individual in the group – I remember there being one group with someone who had worked in international marketing, so they knew everything about bananas or whatever, you know, the food stuff they were working on – so that group member immediately had expert status. And it was very difficult then for the others in the group to challenge that knowledge in any way, to renegotiate what they thought they knew, because this person had first-hand experience. So in a way, although those groups were able to complete the task, they were able to complete the task because of one person in the group who had a strong body of knowledge. In many ways it didn't matter if they didn't know very much.*

Andrew: *Having a little bit of knowledge in this case was quite disruptive. Maybe you pick a subject that nobody knows anything about, like quantum physics or something like that, which would be really interesting ... piecing together understandings and misunderstandings about something like that.*

Donna: *That's one of the things they say about really designing a collaborative learning activity is that it needs to challenge all the learners. Because now if I reflect on it, actually my expectation was that they would produce a map with information on. My expectation would have been better if it was that they got blocked quite early on, because they'd realise they didn't know anything. In many ways, the group that I thought at the time was not achieving the task, I could reverse this and think they were achieving the task. But the problem was that the other groups were further on and that became my expectation. I could have stopped the class after ten minutes and said, 'OK, so what do we do now, now that we recognise that much of what we think we know is based on very little'.*

The dialogue presents an opportunity for Donna to consider her practice through an alternative lens, prompting her to think again, and to reflect on her previous reflection.

Critical issues

Dialogue prompting 'double loop' thinking

Schön (1987, p 31) describes the process as looking back at or considering the thinking that you did while in the midst of action as *'reflection on reflection-in-practice'*. As exemplified in the dialogue above, Donna returns to her earlier reflections on reflection-in-practice. Argyris (1977) describes this as *'double loop'* thinking. Donna has stepped outside the reflective practice cycle and through the dialogue looks back at the activity from a more objective standpoint. Donna is able to challenge her assumptions of accepted practice, disrupting the status quo bias (see Chapter 3). We recognise that being able to reflect on accepted practice is challenging. We do not find it easy to critique our own norms of practice. In this case, the coaching dialogue provided an impetus for double-loop thinking.

Andrew: *Actually, you were trying to get the students to develop some transferable understanding around all sorts of things like teaching and learning, how we work collaboratively, and all of that kind of stuff. The global stuff was kind of irrelevant, but it provided a context. This was about the students learning how to support a group of primary-aged pupils. So, you were modelling, I suppose.*

Donna: *But, you know, now, on reflection, actually, I could critique it quite a lot.*

Donna ends the dialogue on this reflective note. In the following section, we offer seven strategies that lecturers can use to address bias when designing and facilitating learning activities.

Strategies to address biases in learning activities

How can students optimise their learning through learning activities?

In Example 4.1, you read how students can form groups by matching their current knowledge, skills and competencies to the ones needed for the learning activity.

By extending this market-place group formation to include the knowledge, skills and competencies the students would like to develop, they will be engaged in an even more effective self-assessment process. Constructions like continua and bridges provide useful recording resources for self-assessment, visioning and identifying necessary support (Read and Hurford, 2010). For example, students self-assess and record where they are now in terms of their learning at point A on the left-hand side of a continuum or bridge. Next, they vision where they would like to be by the end of the course or learning activity and note this at point B, on the right-hand side of the model. And finally, they label the continuum or the bridge supports with actions and resources they need to enable their learning journey from A to B.

Should we always share LOs?

While it is common practice to share LOs at the start of a class, thereby setting expectations for learning within a framework, might such frameworks limit learning and invite planning fallacy bias and the law of triviality bias to kick in? In Example 4.2, Donna describes a global citizenship activity where the students were expected to engage with a learning activity and then deconstruct it, listing the knowledge, skills and competencies with which they had engaged. The suggestion here is that the teacher still plans the learning activity, so it aligns with the course LOs and assessment, but withholds the specific LOs, leaving these open to the learners' interpretation. If this approach is combined with an expectation that students self-assess and orientate their learning, students would have the opportunity to steer their learning within but also beyond course LOs.

What's the purpose of a learning activity – the learning process or the learning activity's product?

When a learning activity has a pre-defined product outcome, and especially if there is a tight time frame, learners can feel compelled to focus on product completion (Slavin, 2014). Focusing on the product creates parameters or even constraints, which may be necessary for task completion, but they are likely to elicit planning fallacy and the law of triviality biases. Faced with product deadlines, pragmatic students will optimise their limited time, by sharing out the learning activities' tasks among group members to achieve the product outcome. Johnson et al (2014) propose five conditions for collaborative learning: interdependence, self-accountability, group processes, social skills and promotive interaction. If the teacher prioritises processes as much or more than the product when designing the learning activity, they are more likely to facilitate these conditions. All learning activities won't necessarily accommodate all five collaborative learning conditions, but they nevertheless provide a useful checklist and heuristic.

How can learning activities offer ways to develop graduate skills and competencies?

Convincing students to participate in and meaningfully engage with learning activities can be challenging, especially when the activity is not credit-bearing. By reframing learning activities as ways to develop their suite of skills and competencies, we can offer students opportunities to evaluate and enhance their employability. Here we draw on Dacre Pool and Sewell's (2007) holistic model of employability, which extends beyond degree subject knowledge to generic skills, emotional intelligence, development career skills and work experience. The Organisation for Economic Co-operation and Development's three interdisciplinary graduate competencies (OECD, 2019) – creating new value, reconciling tensions and dilemmas and taking responsibility – map well on to the employability model's categories, especially generic skills and emotional intelligence. Universities' employability consultants and educational developers can suggest ways to reframe learning activities so they include opportunities to develop graduate competencies and skills.

How can learning activities help challenge stereotypes?

When designing a learning activity, we can be mindful of how to counter stereotypes through, for example, our choice of images, examples, case studies and references. When supporting an engineering faculty, keen to recruit a more diverse student group, we reviewed how images of students from majority and minority groups can reinforce conceptions of student distribution, roles and responsibilities. To counter these stereotypes, course communication teams can apply diversity and participation criteria when curating photographs of students studying and working. Staff and students are then reassured that they are selecting from a bank of images that show majority and minority students in active and collaborative roles. Similarly, when choosing case studies or examples, it can be helpful to evaluate them against an inclusion heuristic or checklist. For example, the checklist may include the following.

- » Are the roles and responsibilities non-stereotypical or will there be the opportunity to critique stereotypes?
- » Are the context and content accessible and understandable to non-local students?
- » If not, how can the students access relevant information?
- » How can group formation support student engagement with the learning activities?

How can learning activities support threshold concepts?

Threshold concepts are learning building blocks that may be challenging for learners (Meyer and Land, 2003). When planning a learning activity, it is helpful to be clear about its purpose, what it can contribute to the students' learning and whether it provides an opportunity for students to apply their learning about a threshold concept. When learning activities are integrated into taught sessions, they provide opportunities for learners to pause, reflect, question, interact, apply their understanding, evaluate their responses and even hypothesise. All of this engages learners in traversing different taxonomic levels of learning (Anderson et al, 2001). But teachers may be reluctant to allocate teaching time to learning activities and risk reducing the time available for traditional teaching. By focusing learning activities on threshold concepts, teachers can identify clear rationales for the activities (Meyer and Land, 2003). Sometimes it's enough to invite students to use the think, pair, share approach to discuss a threshold concept, and at other times they will need to wrestle with a problem, applying and evaluating their understanding of the concept.

What if students are responsible for resourcing learning activities?

Expecting students to take responsibility for learning from learning activities is a recurrent theme in this chapter's strategies. If we think about resourcing learning activities, teachers often stipulate which resources will be needed or they even provide them, as illustrated in the global citizenship activity. The mapping diagram, which was the product from the learning activity described in the coaching dialogue, only required flip chart paper and marker pens, which Donna provided. What if she hadn't distributed any resources but she had invited the students to find their own ways to map the foods' journeys? Perhaps student groups would have come up with a variety of textual, diagrammatic or even performative ways to share their food maps. As well as adding to the novelty and individualisation of the learning activity and its product, by giving students and student groups ownership over learning activity outcomes and dissemination, we can help offset those unconscious biases which can restrict learning to the most pragmatic and superficial.

Critical questions for practice

» What are the potential risks and benefits of withholding LOs and giving the students the responsibility to deconstruct their learning process and LOs?

» Do we give students too many learning activities? If students are overloaded, does adding to the workload risk precipitating the planning fallacy bias and the law of triviality bias?

» What would encourage students to co-design learning activities? What's in it for them?

Summary

• However committed lecturers may be to inclusive approaches to teaching, there are always opportunities for biases to have an impact.

• Providing learners with opportunities to take ownership can work well, but it is important that lecturers anticipate how learners may respond by, for example, thinking carefully about group composition.

• When lecturers encounter resistance from learners to novel approaches, further reflection may be useful: we touch upon '*reflection on reflection-in-action*' (Schön, 1987) and '*double loop*' thinking (Argyris, 1977).

• We provide some suggestions for how lecturers might think differently about learning activities.

Useful texts

Johnson, David W; **Johnson**, Roger T and **Smith**, Karl A (2014) Cooperative Learning: Improving University Instruction by Basing Practice on Validated Theory. *Journal on Excellence in College Teaching*, 25(3–4): 85–118.

This article reviews five conditions for collaborative learning, which can usefully inform the design of a collaborative learning activity.

Organisation for Economic Co-operation and Development (OECD) (2019) *Transformative Competencies for 2030.* [online] Available at: www.oecd.org/education/2030-project/teaching-and-learning/learning/transformative-competencies/Transformative_Competencies_for_2030_concept_note.pdf (accessed 12 January 2022).

These OECD competencies are informed by current megatrends and signal which competencies students would do well to develop through their education and beyond.

Centre for Teaching and Learning, University of Southern Denmark (2016) *Internationalising the Curriculum, Developing Students Intercultural Competencies. Video – Intercultural Group Work Role Play.* [online] Available at: https://itc.sdu.dk/index.php?page=1.-enabling-intercultural-group-work (accessed 12 January 2022).

The video was developed by three HE students to be used as a resource for teaching about inclusive group work and how perceptions of behaviour can easily provoke biases.

Introduction

In this chapter, we share a typical HE scenario highlighting the variety and disparity of course assessment a student is likely to experience during their undergraduate programme. In order to make sense of the challenges that beset teachers and students when engaging with course assessments, we review current assessment practices and encourage a deeper probing of practices presumed to protect equal opportunities and mitigate biases such as anonymous marking and constructive alignment. Moving between the nexus of theory and practice, we analyse a coaching dialogue between Jack and Ulla. The analysis of the coaching dialogue serves two purposes: to identify and categorise examples of cognitive biases including confirmation bias, functional fixedness and the curse of knowledge bias, and to illustrate how the four-stage coaching model can support a collegial, open dialogue.

Following the analysis, we offer practical ways to prevent or mitigate bias in course and programme assessment. Many of the approaches are interconnected and would be optimised through a programmatic approach but even without this overview they each offer practical strategies for the individual time-pressed teacher.

Theoretical background

Imagine a student on a standard three-year undergraduate degree, studying up to five modules a semester. Each of these modules has its own summative assessment, designed and examined by teachers with their own expectations of student learning and course outcomes. In this scenario, approximately 20 teachers with a diverse range of expectations and experiences could teach and examine any one student's assessments. While a diversity of perspectives may infuse more novelty (Galinsky et al, 2015), a wide range of examiners may also compromise marker reliability and parity of marking (Zahra et al, 2017). And, no matter how constructively aligned module assessments are with the module's LOs, when marking and grading assessments, teachers apply their own norm-referenced '*assessment standards framework*' (Bloxham et al, 2011). These individual frameworks may facilitate the marking process for the teacher, but they may also limit the transparency of the assessment requirements for the students. And if teachers see themselves as 'connoisseurs' of their subjects and their courses (Eisner, 1985) who intuitively know a good assignment when they mark it (Ecclestone, 2001), their tacit knowledge may further limit transparency and parity of marking.

Limited transparency and tacit knowledge are not necessarily indicative of biased marking, but they make it harder to be sure that marking and grading are reliable or that there is parity of student assessment. Transparency is therefore worth pursuing and can be achieved by implementing Assessment for Learning (AfL), including regularly discussing the course assessment, the co-development of assessment criteria, integrating peer feedback and critiquing assessment exemplars (Sadler, 2005). Greater transparency means a clearer shared understanding of the expected standards and a reduction in the gap between the teacher's and the students' expectations.

Critical issues

Questioning the value of anonymous marking

Studies that reveal how cognitive biases, such as stereotype, confirmation and halo biases (see below for explanations of these biases), influence marking and grading provide compelling arguments for anonymous marking of assignments and written exams (Batten et al, 2013; Malouff and Thorsteinsson, 2016) and raise concerns about non-anonymous oral exams and presentations (Roberts et al, 2000; Hazen, 2020). However, alongside these arguments for anonymous marking are studies such as Hinton and Higson's (2017) which found little, if any, change between gender, ethnicity or socio-economic group outcomes after implementing anonymous marking. As noted by the authors (ibid), the findings may be indicative of teachers' increased bias awareness and more inclusive teaching, especially as oral exam performance was seen to improve. Alternatively, we may be looking at another level of marker biases, elicited when confronted with individual students' interpretations of the assessment task. And besides, limited, non-inclusive curricula and traditional assessment modes do little to value diversity and creativity (Bloxham et al, 2011). It's time to challenge the premise that anonymous marking is closing the attainment gap and refocus attention on the wider curricular and assessment experience, especially for the most marginalised students (Pitt and Winstone, 2018).

Curricular and teacher biases need addressing; however, what of students' biases, with their traditional conceptions of effective teaching and learning which can hinder their engagement in constructive pedagogies (Otting et al, 2010)? How do we re-set the norm of *'prevailing assessment cultures'* (McGarr and Clifford, 2013) and convince students of the value of collaborative learning and peer feedback? How do we facilitate their engagement with constructively critical feedback? How can we move a student beyond a sense that the work is good simply because the student believes that it is good? By involving teachers and students in the co-creation of inclusive courses and assessment, we are more likely to increase transparency and address institutional and individual biases (McConlogue, 2020).

Types of bias

The curse of knowledge

We make assumptions about one another. Sometimes this extends to stereotyping and to discrimination. Sometimes it is simply a matter of assuming that others think the same way that we do. Social media has, perhaps, exacerbated this: we move in social bubbles, communicating with people who we have chosen to communicate with because we think they think in the same way that we do. As academics we are, of course, sensitive to the assumptions of others: it is likely that we have all written *'unsubstantiated assertion'* on a student's assignment where we judge that the student has made an assumption about the way the world works, or more precisely an assumption about the way the field in which our expertise is located works. But academics make assumptions too, because academics are people.

In *The Sense of Style*, Pinker (2015) writes about the process of writing, about the language choices that writers make and the difficulty that readers sometimes have in understanding what the writer means. Pinker argues that writers' writing is sometimes incomprehensible because of *'the difficulty of imagining what it's like for someone else not to know something that you know'* (2015, p 57). Pinker describes this as *'the curse of knowledge'* (2015, p 59). We can apply the concept of the curse of knowledge more widely to academic behaviour.

Functional fixedness

We think about objects having a particular function. For example, we put things in a box, we make notes on a piece of paper. Innovation allows us to turn the box over to create a seat or fold the piece of paper to make an aeroplane. Functional fixedness prevents someone from thinking beyond that specific function, limiting innovation or creativity.

Confirmation bias

We look for evidence to support our thinking. Even when we jump to conclusions, we might look for evidence to add weight to that conclusion. Kahneman (2011, p 81) describes the *'deliberate search for confirming evidence'*. The nature of this search depends on what we are aiming to confirm, and we may search for evidence that allows us to confirm a particular conclusion. This is confirmation bias. If a particular conclusion has already been pointed out to us, that might push us towards seeking evidence to confirm this conclusion, without first challenging the veracity or significance of this conclusion.

The following extracts from the dialogue between Jack and Ulla illustrate how the GROW model helped elicit these biases.

Using dialogue to identify bias in approaches to assessment

The dialogue: context and structure

The participants were Jack, who asked the questions, and Ulla, who responded. The dialogue focused on an undergraduate written assignment. The participants have substantial experience in HE. Shared understanding of HE systems will have affected the shape and features of the dialogue. In an informal conversation at the start of the dialogue, the participants agreed that strict adherence to the GROW formula might not be helpful: the obstacles and challenges of assessment in HE were too nuanced for strict adherence to the GROW question stems to be effective. The *Goal* question ('What do you want?') was not adapted. The participants agreed that the *Reality* question ('Where are you now?') was too vague. The *Reality* question was adapted to 'In your position as the marker, what knowledge do you have about the module and the assessment? What can you share with me to unpack the module?' Jack angles the *Options* question obliquely: 'You probably can't do anything for the current cohort now – what do you learn from this experience that might be useful to take forward?' Ulla's response takes the dialogue into the realm of *Will Do* without Jack having to ask the question.

Unpacking the dialogue

| Goal question | > | Jack: | *What would you like to get from the next 30 minutes?* |

Ulla: *The challenge I have, having completed module marking, is to know that the process has been fair. I want to explore strategies which I could use, things I could have done differently or perhaps find affirmation that what I have done is okay, that the outcomes were inevitable*

Jack: *So, you have clarified your goal to identify what you may have been able to do differently and possibly affirmation that what you did do was the right thing to do.*

Ulla: *Yes.*

Jack: *In your position as the marker, what knowledge do you have about the module and the assessment? What can you share with me to unpack the module?*

Ulla: *I am the module leader. It's my assignment: I designed it, prepared the resources, and have taught it for five years. I have adapted the support guidance, the ways of framing the assignment for students each year in response to questions from students, which suggests areas of confusion and uncertainty. This is a Level 6 assignment, so I also have expectations of students being able to resolve things for themselves independently. I see problem solving and independence as graduate-type skills. It's important there's a degree of autonomy.*

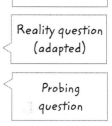

Jack mirrors what Ulla says, reusing some of her language. Note the reuse of 'affirmation'.

Reality question (adapted)

Probing question

Ulla has clear expectations. She expects students in the final year of an undergraduate course to be able to work things out for themselves, to be independent. She sees these as the skills that prospective graduates should have; we might concur. She wants the assessment process to be 'fair'; this is something we all might aspire to.

This extract also suggests that the curse of knowledge is present in Ulla's thinking and that she applies this when marking students' work. Specifically, she feels that prospective graduates should have certain skills or attributes although Ulla has not shared her expectations with students via the assessment criteria nor made them explicit in the assignment brief. Ulla's responses suggest that she thinks she knows how evidence of these skills or attributes will be manifested in students' submissions. Here then, there is a double layer of implicit teacher expectations: students at this level should know that they ought to be competent problem-solvers and independent thinkers, *and* they should know how to demonstrate this in a 3000-word essay.

The issues around implicit expectations are further complicated by Ulla's sense of ownership of the module: her response suggests that for her the module, the assignment and the associated resources are effective. This appears to be a type of functional fixedness: she has spent five years with this module and her capacity to innovate is, potentially, limited. There are also shades of the IKEA effect (see Chapter 2): Ulla built this module, so she believes it is necessarily good.

Later in this part of the dialogue, Jack picks up a thread about differences in attainment and notes that Ulla has expressed concern about 'sensitive marking'. *Sensitive marking is an accommodation to remove barriers for students with specific learning needs. For example, sensitive marking might involve less emphasis on grammatical accuracy.*

> Clarification: context and processes

Jack: *What are your concerns about sensitive marking?*

Ulla: *The e-learning platform flags the submissions of students 'eligible for sensitive marking'. The implication of this is that the marker won't pick up every grammatical or spelling error, granting some flexibility to the student. But given I may anticipate that these students won't do so well, perhaps the 'sensitive marking' label prompts lower expectations on my part.*

Ulla acknowledges that confirmation bias may be present here. The sensitive marking flag draws to her attention the possibility that this submission may not be as strong as another, unflagged submission. As assessors mark, they may look for evidence in the submission that confirms that this relative weakness is the case.

The dialogue returns to expectations later.

> Use of language: although the dialogue addresses bias, Jack does not explicitly use the term bias. This may be deliberate and may lead to a more open set of responses.

Jack: *The students getting lower marks this year, is there a pattern, in how they use literature, the structure of assignments?*

Ulla: *To an extent, definitely structure. Where structure obscures clarity of meaning. For example, in a paragraph as a reader you need a sense of what's going to be there, there might be a topic sentence indicating the content of the paragraph, signposting. But where that doesn't happen you'll end up somewhere completely different. I felt that I'd provided input on this at an appropriate level.*

Jack: *You probably can't do anything for the current cohort now – what do you learn from this experience that might be useful to take forward?*

Options question

Ulla: *There is something I can do for this cohort because this was a semester 1 module and I also teach them for a semester 2 module. This tells me what the weaknesses of some students are and that's already informing my delivery: I know that for some students finding literature and engaging with literature and communicating about literature is more challenging. But they will all benefit if I embed training in these skills in the module.*

Response flows into Will Do

This dialogue has raised a number of bias-related challenges in assessment practice. Below we have listed nine strategies, inspired by inclusive HE practices which teachers can employ to address bias in assessment.

Strategies to address biases in assessment

Designing course assessment

Course assessments provide opportunities for learners to show what they have learnt and the quality of their learning. To be clear for students and teachers that the assessment is designed to assess the course's LOs, course assessments and course LOs need to be aligned. However, other factors, such as time allocated for marking, preferred assessment methods and other resource provisions, frequently influence decisions over assessment design. By prioritising an integrated approach to assessment, each course's assessment is checked for its alignment with the course LOs and its contribution to a holistic programme of study.

Choosing the fairest assessment method

When considering fairness, a useful starting point is whether the assessment method is fit for purpose. The SMARTER model (Lawlor and Hornyak, 2012) provides a framework for the design of behavioural LOs which can be 'measured' by an assessment method. See below for an exemplification of how SMARTER can provide an effective checklist when selecting an assessment method.

Example 5.1

Selecting an assessment method

When course assessments comprise written assignments, the marker may be influenced by the quality of the composition, including the writing style, vocabulary, spelling and referencing even if these are not explicitly addressed in the assignment's LOs. When reviewing assessment strategies, it is worth agreeing how composition, writing style and the secretarial elements of the submission will be assessed. At course level, you could generate a series of graduated feedback statements for written submissions, such as: 'The writing style is coherent and clear, and ensures that the reader can readily access the writer's meaning' or 'The assignment is written in a clear and accessible way; mistakes in grammar or spelling do not limit the reader's understanding of the writer's message'. To ensure parity of marking, co-marking a range of assignments will help identify differences in marker expectations; revisiting portfolios of benchmarked assignments will reinforce the importance of parity and the application of the SMARTER checklist.

Clarifying and practising assessment expectations

Teachers who commit course time to developing shared understanding of what is required by a course assessment are clearly signaling the importance of clarifying assessment expectations. By giving students the opportunity to review assessment exemplars and apply course criteria, teachers are giving students the role of course examiner. Through the collaborative peer review process, students learn to critically evaluate a peer's work and to negotiate the provision of constructive feedback and feed forward. The peer review process is professionalised and de-personalised by the provision of checklists and rubrics which facilitate criteria-aligned assessment and feedback.

Critical issues

Institutional assessment practices: 'eligible for sensitive marking'

HEIs' assessment practices may be intended to ensure equal opportunities; however, such practices may not be informed by more recent findings on structural and hierarchical biases (Noon, 2018) and anonymous marking (Hinton and Higson, 2017). Awareness of the contested findings from anonymous and institutional practices can help markers recognise how other biases associated with literacy or presentation style, and composition may influence their assessments. HEIs' 'sensitive marking' procedures, designed to ensure students with learning needs are not penalised for style or composition errors, may however invoke markers' low expectations and lead them to apply a 'glass ceiling' or a tacit limit on their grading. An alternative approach would be to replace signalling specific eligible cases with universal 'sensitive marking'.

When marking written assignments

Examiners are found to rely on their internalised assessment standards frameworks rather than direct reference to assessment criteria. These internalised frameworks may become more nuanced, tacit and possibly biased as an examiner develops their marking experience and expertise.

Using checklists or rubrics when marking written assignments

To mitigate possible biases, examiners can provide feedback using the module's assessment checklist or rubric. If there is a team of examiners, the course leader can mark a few assignments and share their initial marking with the team, inviting dialogue and an agreed decision on benchmarking and criteria weighting. Examiners may norm reference to offset their confirmation biases; however, a final review of assignments on grading borderlines will help ensure criteria referencing is being observed.

When assessing through presentations and oral exams

Carefully planned, constructively aligned oral questioning with on-the-spot clarification checks and scaffolded probing questions can provide unique opportunities for students to excel. However, visual and auditory cues may trigger confirmation biases stemming from prior knowledge of the student's performance in class or due to the invocation of stereotype biases (see Chapter 2).

Example 5.2

Following a checklist of inclusive practices can help mitigate potential biases in performative exams. The *Oral Exam Checklist for Bias Aware Assessment* offers guidance for lecturers preparing students for an oral exam and guidance for their own practice before, during and after the exam when grading the quality of a student's exam contribution (Hurford, 2020). The checklist includes a version of the self-checking flipping perceptions technique, where the examiners ask themselves '*if this student* (include a visual or auditory difference, e.g. sounded more confident, looked more engaged ...), *how would I react?*'

When assessing group assignments

Group assignments can engage students with authentic learning and assessment and help them hone their interpersonal graduate competencies. When assessing group assignments, all parties must be clear whether individual or group grades are the outcome. Making groups responsible for co-ordinating and confirming their individual and combined contributions with a cover note listing each group member's contributions, accompanied by peer signatures, professionalises the group-work process. However, when marking well-integrated group assignments, it is challenging to extricate individual grades. An alternative is to award a common grade for the group assignment and grade individual reflections on the group assignment's process or outcome. Each student's grade would then reflect their contributions to a collaborative assessment and an individual assessment.

When assessing portfolios

Portfolio assessments can maintain student engagement with the whole course and motivate them to self-assess and criteria-align the selection of their assignment items. However, unless criteria are well aligned, the range of portfolio items can be challenging and time-consuming to assess with a risk of low reliability and markers' biased preferences. These concerns can be mitigated through a teacher/student collaboration on the design of portfolio assessments, peer review processes to support portfolio item selection, and individual reflections on the course's learning and assessment processes illustrated by appended portfolio items. If the grading is then weighted towards the reflection rather than the portfolio items, the examiner can clarify their focus.

Marking under pressure

Time-pressed examiners need to adopt pragmatic approaches to marking without compromising fairness and criteria referencing. Courses can be planned to spread the assessment load across the modules, avoiding final assessment overload for the marker and students. Interspersing assessments in a module enables purposeful formative feedback and feedforward which supports the final submission. Alternatively, if the summative assessment is fixed at the module end, the assessment method needs to be SMARTER and time-efficient. Methods like multiple-choice questions with well-planned question stems, group assignments with group or individual oral exams, or exams with criteria-aligned questions, combined with checklists and rubrics, can aid time saving and keep the marking process focused.

Co-assessing with internal or external examiners

Quality assurance is often the primary purpose for co-assessing with another examiner, although the impartiality of a co-assessor is not always evident (Bloxham and Price, 2015). HEIs' assessment protocol generally provides guidance on roles and responsibilities, which can then be discussed by co-examiners to ensure shared understanding and agreement. It is advisable to share and discuss all assessment resources with the co-examiner. During performative exams, it then falls to the teacher to explain how they and the co-examiner will facilitate the exam and to follow those practices. When discussing assignments or exam performance, referring to the course assessment rubric or criteria checklist for clarification and confirmation of proposed grades and feedback can help ensure a fair and criteria-referenced assessment process.

Critical questions for practice

» How do we manage our own biases when engaging in course assessment?

» Why would we engage in a coaching dialogue about assessment? What would have happened to make this feel necessary?

» What agency do we have to mitigate the effects of bias on assessment? How much flexibility does our institution allow?

Summary

- Bias is present in everyone's practice: awareness of this and the capacity to identify and challenge it is vital.

- Critical dialogues such as the one explored in this chapter work where they are open and free from judgement.

- Critical dialogues where practitioners have opportunities to identify solutions for themselves can be particularly effective.

- It is important to remember that anonymous assessment is not a panacea for equal opportunities and unbiased assessment.

- Institutional mechanisms, such as sensitive marking, are often well-intentioned, but examination of these processes should form part of the critical dialogue.

Useful texts

Hinton, Daniel P and **Higson**, Helen (2017) A Large-Scale Examination of the Effectiveness of Anonymous Marking in Reducing Group Performance Differences in Higher Education Assessment. *PLoS ONE*, 12(8): e0182711. [online] Available at: https://journals.plos.org/plosone/article?id=10.1371/journal.pone.0182711 (accessed 13 January 2022).

This research study's findings challenge the assumption that anonymous marking addresses assessment gaps and facilitates unbiased marking.

Malouff, John and **Thorsteinsson**, Einer B (2016) Bias in Grading: 'A Meta-analysis of Experimental Research Findings'. *Australian Journal of Education*, 60(3): 245–56.

This research study provides a compelling argument for anonymous marking as a way to address biased marking.

Chapter 6 | Structural and institutional biases

Introduction

The focus on institutional bias reveals the systemic prevalence of discriminatory processes which affect institutional identity and practices such as marketing, recruitment and promotion, curriculum, resourcing, pedagogy, services and student outcomes. In the opening section of this chapter, we discuss how discriminatory processes have enabled the perpetuity of the status quo bias which significantly limits the number of BAME academic staff, especially at professor levels. We note how stereotype threat bias insidiously limits diversity in recruitment and how bias blind spot (see Chapter 2) can enable institutions like HEIs to make self-evaluation judgements that paint practice in an inaccurately positive light. This chapter's coaching dialogue between Sanne and Faisal, both in HE management positions, reveals the complexity of unconscious bias both in its manifestations and its effects. As Sanne and Faisal's dialogue develops, they touch on status quo bias (see Chapter 3) and marking; they share an unexpected IKEA effect bias (see Chapter 2) with regard to student effort and highlight how stereotyping and the bias blind spot leads to the problematic homogenisation of groups of students with widely different strengths and needs, more easily referred to as BAME and first-generation students. We advocate HEIs use their social capital and academic capabilities to deepen societal understanding of prejudice and bias, and to provide an institutional lead by implementing sustained and holistic commitment to addressing institutional bias.

Theoretical background

Chapters 2–5 of this book are designed to support individual lecturers in their quest for bias-aware teaching, learning and assessment. However, this chapter sets the HE scene by focusing on institutional bias. By institutional bias we are referring to systemic biases which are rooted in institutional operations and practices and by default exert their influence over institutional identity and practices, including marketing, recruitment and promotion, curriculum, resourcing, pedagogy and services (Arday, 2015). Institutional practices are prone to status quo bias (see Chapter 3): how often do we hear the remark *'That's the way we do it here'*, or *'We have always done it this way'*? In the UK we only have to look to the Higher Education Statistics Agency data for 2019/20 (2021) to remind ourselves of the impact of status quo bias on staff recruitment: *'fewer than 1% of university professors are black'* (Adams, 2020). And while

HEIs are often committed to overturning systemic bias, more fundamental action to challenge and shift this is clearly required:

University institutions have themselves proved remarkably resilient to change in terms of curriculum, culture and staffing, remaining for the most part 'ivory towers' – with the emphasis on 'ivory'.
(Alexander and Arday, 2015, p 4)

'*Racial disadvantage remains stubbornly persistent*' (Pilkington, 2018, p 28) in UK HEIs, a fact compounded by the 13 per cent attainment gap (or degree-awarding gap) in high-level undergraduate degree classifications for BAME students compared with white British students (Amos and Doku, 2019a). Therefore, if institutional bias is not identified, addressed and replaced with equitable, unbiased processes and systems, status quo bias will prevail, thereby limiting graduate and academic opportunities. What incentive is there for students and colleagues to pursue education or an academic career in a HE environment which is systemically biased against their entitlement and opportunities because of their ethnicity?

The institutional status quo can also compromise and even undermine individual efforts to address bias at course or programme level. For example, an HE lecturer's teaching about recruitment and meritocracy will lack institutional authenticity and valid role models if the HEI's staff and student recruitment systems are algorithmically biased towards the stereotype threat bias (Donovan et al, 2018). The stereotype threat bias is present when we are influenced by societal, cultural, institutional norms to the exclusion of meritocracy (Reay, 2018). For example, a diverse panel of interviewers may still appoint a candidate who fits the *white Western male* norm because they cannot mediate the effect of their unconscious bias towards the stereotypical *preferred* candidate (Moss-Racusin et al, 2012). Furthermore, unless individual actions have a sustained, co-ordinated focus they are unlikely to address systemic, institutional bias.

There are different biases that are likely to affect institutional practice. We have already mentioned stereotype threat and status quo bias which can reinforce patterns of institutional behaviour. A further bias example is bias blind spot (Pronin and Kugler, 2007), evident in self-evaluation processes where we tend to evaluate ourselves introspectively, while evaluating others behaviourally (see Chapter 2). For example, Donna, one of the authors of this book, might make the following introspective observation: '*I'm a woman – how can I possibly be sexist?*' This might then lead to the self-evaluative conclusion: '*I am not sexist*'. And Donna might compound this self-belief by comparing herself with others and applying different metrics: she evaluates others by their sexist behaviours, a metric she does not apply to herself. The application of these different metrics reinforces our bias blind spot and leads us to self-evaluation judgements that are more positive than our evaluation judgements of others.

Example 6.1

Mandatory unconscious bias training

In this example we apply a bias blind spot to an HEI. An HEI evaluates high staff participation in mandatory unconscious bias training as a successful initiative and outcome: box ticked. This success story can be publicised and help reinforce an institutional perception of achievement against diversity and bias awareness criteria. However, unless this training is integrated into a holistic and sustained commitment to addressing bias and supporting initiatives that create a more equitable academic environment (Amos and Doku, 2019a), stand-alone unconscious bias training is unlikely to reduce bias (Atewologun et al, 2018). And because we are biased towards feeling comfortable, such training may entrench participants' biases (Munch-Jurisic, 2020). Any institution which regards mandatory bias or diversity training as the solution is at best deluding itself and at worst risking sustaining rather than addressing bias (Noon, 2018).

Types of bias

This chapter's dialogue touches on a range of biases impacting on institution-wide approaches and on individual interpretations of these approaches. We touch upon an instance of the IKEA effect, albeit one that offers an unusual perspective of this. Bias blind spot emerges as a hazard in assignment marking. It is possible that this links to evidence of status quo bias, in the sense that *this is how it has always been and always will be*.

Using dialogue to identify structural and institutional bias

Dialogue: context and structure

Sanne, a university department director, talks with Faisal, a senior academic manager. They both work in post-'92 universities. In the UK, post-'92 universities (established as universities after 1992) are former polytechnics, often focusing on vocational courses and with an explicit commitment to widening participation, targeting marketing materials at, for example, applicants with diverse learning needs.

Unpacking the dialogue

<table>
<tr>
<td>

Reality
question 1

</td>
<td>

Sanne:

</td>
<td>

I know that you've worked at other universities: is there something about post-'92 universities where there is a sense of needing to be really tough, really demonstrating that standards are unquestionably high, concerned to show that we're doing 'the right thing'?

</td>
</tr>
</table>

Faisal: *Yeah, absolutely. I worked at another post-'92 university and there we had similar ways of doing things. I feel that when we mark work now, for example, people really reluctantly use the whole of the marking scale. I include myself. Getting an 85 is such a rarity here. But I've looked at really good pieces of work and thought, 'Well, what else could the student have done? And you've only given it a 72'. Even feedback from the external examiners here and at my previous institution was: 'Use the whole marking scale. Don't be afraid to give an 85. No one is saying give 100 but don't be afraid to give an 85'. You would give a 5: I've given a 5 to a student who just did a couple of lines or something like that. But then don't be afraid to go further to the top end. We know 70 is a first, but you know, if somebody's done an exceptional piece of work, we should acknowledge this in the grade.*

Without a clear institution-wide expectation for markers to use the full spectrum of grades, it is likely that the status quo in relation to marking within a narrow range described by Faisal will persist. Status quo bias is the tendency to avoid change. In this case, if markers have habitually set the ceiling at 72 (or even 85), the shift to a wider spectrum of marks carries risk: accusations of excessive generosity, loss of reputation ('*She's a tough marker*'), loss of a sense that the approach employed for years was 'best practice'. Kahneman writes that '*animals, including people, fight harder to prevent losses than to achieve gains*' (2011, p 305). Change carries the risk that things will deteriorate rather than improve as a consequence: a clear institution-wide steer would be a way to shift this.

Critical issues

Factors fuelling the status quo

The desire to maintain the status quo may be unconsciously fuelled by other factors and sustained by a lack of consistent institution-wide policy or guidance. For example, the marker may rely on intuition when grading work: we know markers rely on their tacit knowledge about a subject when marking and rarely refer to assessment criteria (Bloxham et al, 2011). In turn, this instinct may be fed by the marker's unconscious beliefs about the capacity of the students they teach: *'This is a really good essay, but I can't see how students at this university could get a grade higher than 72'*. Or it might be that the marker's thinking is swayed by their status as an expert in the field coupled with their own academic history: *'As an undergraduate, I never got more than 72, so why should I grade any higher than that today?'* Perhaps marking is swayed by an embedded tendency to distribute grades in line with the Bell Curve: *'This is a really good essay, but I've already given another essay 80, so I'll need to think carefully about the overall distribution of marks'*. And of course, thoughts about the distribution of marks at both ends of the spectrum can preoccupy markers. All of these factors are characteristic of the impact of bias blind spot, where the marker is influenced by a norm not shared with the students. What strategies can HEIs employ to unearth and effectively challenge the status quo?

Faisal continues: *And especially when writing that final-year undergraduate project which is the biggest piece of work any student has ever done up to that point. The student has put more time into this than anything else they've ever done; I feel like feedback sometimes expects too much. I've seen feedback which says, 'Oh, but you didn't consider X, Y and Z'. But this is an undergraduate project, not a PhD. If they didn't consider X, Y and Z it's because they couldn't do it in 9000 words.*

Securing 'fairness' in marking is fraught with challenge. We have flagged some of the biases that may confine grades awarded within tight boundaries. The IKEA effect (see Chapter 2) leaves the creator (of a piece of assessed work, for example) with an exaggerated sense of the worth of the thing created because of the time and effort invested in its creation. It is interesting here how the IKEA effect impacts on Faisal's consideration of the marking of the third-year project. The project is *'the biggest piece of work any student has ever done up to that point. The student has put more time into this than anything else they've ever done'* – Faisal implies that this warrants more generous (or less exacting) marking as a consequence.

Critical issues

Institution-wide standardisation

What opportunities are there to standardise marking across subjects? HEI quality assurance mechanisms are designed to ensure that courses are validated in line with HE-wide standards. These processes are often supported by external examiners whose role is to bring a cross-sector perspective, although Bloxham and Price (2015) question the impartiality of external examiners. But how does the HEI ensure that, for example, a second-year undergraduate engineering submission is as worthy of an 85 as a second-year undergraduate history submission? And what about those marks between 85 and 100? Are STEM subject lecturers more or less likely than social science lecturers, for example, to use the whole range?

Later, the dialogue moves on to the ways that a commitment to widening participation may impact on policy and practice.

| Reality question 2 | Sanne: | *Is there a sense that 'the sort of students that come to post-'92 universities' need a particular kind of approach?* |

| Option identified | Faisal: | *We talk a lot about first-generation students whose parents haven't gone to university, or students who might be the first in their family to go to university.* |

We say, 'Therefore, they need this. Therefore, they need that'. I don't think anyone actually knows what the students need. I don't think anyone's actually gone to a student at a post-'92 university and said, 'Are you a first-generation student? Have your parents gone to university? Have your brothers or sisters gone to university? What do you need?' I think the student would be like, 'What are you talking about?'

Henderson et al (2020) found that students who are the first in their family to attend university are '*less likely to attend Russell Group universities than their peers with university-educated parents*' and are '*more likely to drop out than students whose parents have a degree*' (2020, p 748). What Faisal is concerned about is that this cohort of 'first in family' students are thought of as a homogenous entity.

Sanne: *So that's stereotyping, thinking about a whole group of people who are first in family as if they're all the same. One wise professor once said, 'If you've met one person with autism, you've met one person with autism'. We could apply the same here: each student who happens to be the first in their family to come to university will be different to any other student who is first to come to university. Each student will have their own 'stuff'.*

Sanne recognises the way that stereotypes can narrow the way in which we think about addressing inequality. There is a danger that the individual 'gets lost' in our conceptualisation of the group as a homogenous entity. In order to make sense of issues, we circumvent complexity by using shortcuts in the form of stereotypes and simplistic labels.

Critical issues

What's in a name?

We can also apply this thinking to a critique of the use of the term Black, Asian and minority ethnic (BAME), widely used in UK schools, colleges and universities. The term BAME is seen by many as reductive (Alexander, 2017) so not fit for purpose. Today, the term continues to imply *otherness*, the shared characteristic of being *not white*. Even as universities use the term conditionally, acknowledging the diversity and distinctiveness BAME covers, its continued use allows universities to measure and plan to address inequality as if BAME students were a homogenous body. How does your university develop nuance in its management of inequality?

Sanne: *Do you think there is a bias blind spot here? Might it be that post-'92 universities think 'Because of the cohorts of students that come here – first generation at university, high proportion of BAME students – we're good at supporting, facilitating, enabling a particular "type" of student'?*

> Sanne attempts to push Faisal towards a particular conclusion

Faisal: *I don't think that's the assumption. I think that it's more about an attempt to make it part of the identity of the university, this whole widening participation angle. That we are the university for this type of student. 'We are here for widening participation'.*

It is interesting that Faisal and Sanne see this differently. It may be that the identity of an institution – its unique selling point, the way it presents itself to *the market* – is not aligned with the experience or outcomes achieved. But if this were the case it would suggest that there is cognitive dissonance at play: by making 'widening participation' a key pillar of its identity, the university *implies* that those students who come from non-traditional backgrounds (first in family, mature students, BAME students and so on) will succeed. If this espoused commitment (albeit espoused only by implication) is not aligned with actual outcomes, there will be institutional tension. What are your university's implicit or explicit commitments? To what extent does your university meet these commitments? How do you know?

The dialogue ends with some thoughts about what *success* means.

Faisal: *For some of our students – I'm making an assumption here – but I think for some of our students, coming to university and getting a degree is 'success'. We might measure success differently. But just getting to the end of the degree for some of these students will be a big deal.*

Sanne: *I've had conversations with undergraduate students about this over the last couple of years. And often, very often, they have little notion of what 'a graduate job' is. The aspiration is to have a degree, to graduate. That is the thing. 'Nobody in my family has done this thing before. I'm the first person in my family to have a degree'. The employability data really fails to acknowledge this. You know, 'you must have a graduate job for it somehow to be of ...'*

Faisal: *Value. We're placing the value here – well the government links the value of the degree to what job it gets you. And that is really problematic because, if that's the way it is, it will drive out subjects where there is not a clear employment pathway.*

Example 6.2

Measuring 'success' in UK higher education

UK universities are ranked in a number of ways. League tables, developed and published by newspapers such as *The Guardian* and *The Times*, use a range of metrics to calculate league position. *The Guardian*, for example, includes metrics linked to career prospects and calculates a value-added score based on the percentage of students leaving with a *good degree*, ie a 1st or a 2:1. The 'Teaching Excellence Framework' (TEF), which awards UK universities Bronze, Silver or

Gold status, includes in the calculation data on graduates' engagement in highly skilled employment or further study following graduation. This can influence HEI decisions about the range of courses offered – are some degree courses more likely to lead to highly skilled employment? – and asks all involved in the sector *'What is the purpose of a university education?'*

HEIs will find themselves pulled in different directions, sometimes leading to dissonance between policy and practice. Of course, when we write about HEI decisions, about HEI policy and HEI practice, we are really writing about the human decision-makers: individuals working at various levels within HE who, to a greater or lesser extent, will have agency to address structural and institutional biases. Below we have listed strategies that lecturers, researchers, personnel managers and institutional leaders can employ to address structural and institutional biases.

Strategies to address structural and institutional biases

Cross-faculty marking dialogues

Second marking by a co-lecturer or a colleague familiar with a subject is common HEI practice. However, while the shared subject knowledge is advantageous when checking for the accuracy and depth of subject knowledge, there is a risk of confirmation bias. What if we held inter-faculty coaching dialogues about marking and grading assessments? In this way, a lecturer from Faculty A, who is a non-subject specialist for courses offered by Faculty B, asks the Faculty B lecturer a series of scaffolded questions, designed to keep the marker alert to possible influences on their marking. These questions could include the following.

» How are you applying the assessment criteria?

» How are you weighting the criteria and why?

» What do you do when the assessed work straddles two grades?

» What are the external factors influencing your marking, such as student evaluations, Bell Curve expectations and your reputation as a marker?

» What is the evidence in the work for the final grade?

» What feedforward will you give the student?

The lecturers could either swap roles when the Faculty A lecturer is marking or they would draw a different marking dialogue partner from a pool.

Closing the attainment gap

Amos and Doku's (2019a) *Closing the Gap* report explains the persistence of the attainment gap in UK HEIs and its impact on BAME students' university experiences and graduate outcomes. The report includes five institutional strategies, listed below, designed to address the attainment or degree awarding gap for BAME students:

1. *strong leadership;*
2. *having conversations about race and changing the culture;*
3. *developing racially diverse and inclusive environments;*
4. *getting the evidence and analysing the data;*
5. *understanding what works.*

(Amos and Doku, 2019a)

The report provides a clear rationale for implementing these five strategies in UK HEIs, and each strategy is explained and illustrated with examples of UK HEI practices. The report includes a helpful checklist, 'Table 1: Checklist of Actions' (ibid, p 32), with questions for consideration and suggested actions followed by possible barriers to success and associated questions and actions. The HEI examples for each strategy are further developed in the accompanying *Closing the Gap* collection of case studies (Amos and Doku, 2019b). These two documents provide clear institutional and individual guidance on how to address discriminatory bias and practices in pursuit of inclusive and racially diverse environments.

Bias and artificial intelligence

Artificial intelligence (AI) is regarded by some as the solution to human bias, but as AI researcher at Microsoft Kate Crawford reveals, this is far from the case (Corbyn, 2021). The bias in AI may come from the designers' own biases or the stereotypical data set that is fed into the algorithm to train it to do its job. In practice this means that if the data set replicates the current recruitment norm or stereotypical criteria, for example a white western male for a professor position, then the algorithm will only be equipped to apply that norm. Recruitment or promotion selection which relies upon AI will be biased towards its data set, and '*some algorithms privilege a certain group of people over another*' (Donovan et al, 2018, p 3). Who is responsible for algorithm accountability? If an HEI uses AI to support its recruitment processes, what checks and balances does the institution have in place to be assured that decisions are unbiased? Such questions need to be addressed by recruitment and personnel teams, and students or staff applying for HEI places and positions need to be assured that their applications are being fairly evaluated.

Call for HEIs to take the lead addressing bias

We know too little about what reduces or even dispels prejudice (Palluck and Green, 2009): therein lies the problem with unconscious bias training (Atewologun et al, 2018; Noon, 2018). As highlighted in this chapter's first critical issue on mandatory unconscious bias training, putting the emphasis on individuals addressing their own biases will not address institutional or societal biases and may lead to entrenched bias. Noon (2018) argues we must address bias at institutional and societal levels because unconscious influences stem from '*social contexts and can only be challenged by social action*' (Noon, 2018, p 205). He advocates for sociologists and critical organisational theorists to critique the '*narrative of unconscious bias*' (Noon, 2018, p 200) and thereby deepen and widen our understanding of how it influences our decisions. HEIs have the research capacity to pursue relevant research. HEI leadership and research-funding bodies are in the optimum position to enable and prioritise research into understanding and addressing bias. In addition, national and international HE organisations can facilitate networks to forefront the research findings. Most importantly, HE organisations can ensure that findings are actioned rather than shelved until the next government requirement to address biased practices and unequal opportunities and outcomes for HE students and staff (Pilkington, 2018).

Critical questions for practice

» How impartial is assessment practice in your course, department or institution? How do you know?

» To what extent are students at your institution thought of as individuals or as homogenous groups?

» What is the *mission* or *vision* of your institution? To what extent is this reflected in student outcomes? How do you know?

» How can you work collaboratively across your course or department to unearth and mitigate the impacts of institution-wide bias?

Summary

- Systemic bias continues to impact HEI policy and practice.

- Embedded institutional bias, reflected for example in lecturer recruitment or student outcomes, will compromise individuals' attempts to challenge or overcome bias.

- Explicit progressive institution-wide expectations and inter-departmental collaboration relating to, for example, assessment practice are crucial if the impacts of structural and institutional biases are to be challenged and overturned.

- Institution-wide understanding of the full implications of institutional mission statements or vision statements is a positive first step towards aligning what institutions espouse with students' actual experience and success.

Useful texts

Amos, Valerie and **Doku**, Amatey (2019a) Black, Asian and Minority Ethnic Student Attainment at UK Universities: Closing the Gap. [online] Available at: www.universitiesuk.ac.uk/policy-and-analysis/reports/Pages/bame-student-attainment-uk-universities-closing-the-gap.aspx (accessed 13 January 2022).

This report provides a rationale for addressing the attainment gap and a list of five institutional strategies to address bias and discriminatory practices, which can affect BAME students' student experiences and university outcomes.

Amos, Valerie and **Doku**, Amatey (2019b) Black, Asian and Minority Ethnic Student Attainment at UK Universities: #Closing the Gap. Case Studies. [online] Available at: www.universitiesuk.ac.uk/sites/default/files/field/downloads/2021-09/bame-student-attainment-uk-universities-case-studies.pdf (accessed 13 January 2022).

This compilation of case studies from UK HEIs provides examples of institutional practices, informed by the accompanying report's five strategies. The case studies were designed to address bias and discriminatory practices which were affecting BAME students' student experiences and university outcomes.

Arday, Jason and **Mirza**, Heidi Safa (eds) (2018) *Dismantling Race in Higher Education: Racism, Whiteness and Decolonising the Academy.* London: Palgrave.

This edited book includes uncompromising studies of the current situation in UK HEIs as experienced by BAME academic staff and students.

While reviewing the book in preparation for this chapter, we felt compelled to offer a final dialogue that embraces a HE role wherein all the chapters are simultaneously relevant. This led us to discuss how this book could support a recently appointed course leader and the multiple, interconnecting challenges they face when addressing different expectations by the course teachers and the students; hence the final coaching dialogue between Pete, a new course leader, and Sue, an educational developer. Here we tease out some of those complexities bound up in students' anonymised feedback via a national evaluation survey and how a course leader might engage with the feedback and their course team in fair and unbiased ways.

Types of bias

This dialogue focuses on a course leader's reflections on student feedback. A number of biases that we have discussed previously are evident, including stereotyping, the IKEA effect, bias blind spot and status quo bias.

Using dialogue to identify a web of biases

Dialogue: context and structure

Sue, an educational developer at an HEI, talks with Pete, who has been asked to look at recent course feedback (see Table 7.1).

Dialogue as a tool to address multiple challenges

Previously in this book, we have identified individual critical issues arising from each dialogue. The dialogue in this chapter unearths a range of biases, discussed elsewhere in the book. But the challenge of reflecting on and resolving a network of challenges perhaps more closely mirrors the experience of those working in HE, especially for someone in a course management role.

Table 7.1 An excerpt from students' free-text feedback comments

Positive	Negative
The assignment brief for the second module in the third year was really clear, with a clear structure to follow.	Some of my friends got higher marks for work that was no better than my work. They agreed with me: my work was just good as theirs.
Some of the lecturers were really engaging. I definitely learnt the most from ****.	Lots of the seminars were a waste of time. **** would give us an activity and nobody knew what to do, so we'd just talk about other stuff. They should have been teaching us not just leaving us to work it out for ourselves. I mean, that's what we pay the fees for.
I started working in September and I am using many of the skills I developed on the course in my new role.	Limited spaces to eat lunch, and no access to a microwave.
The library staff were brilliant – and the library was open 24/7. Some of the lecturers would reply to emails really quickly, even at the weekend.	We were expected to prepare for sessions and sometimes the readings weren't shared until the last minute. Some lecturers seemed to think we could just drop everything for university stuff, but I had a job and needed to spend time with my kids.

Unpacking the dialogue

Sue: *What's your goal for our meeting today?*

Pete: *I'd like to have some clear ideas about how to address some of the negative points from the course feedback and just want to have a chance to talk about the context that maybe led to some of these less positive comments.*

> Goal question

Sue: *What's your current situation? Maybe talk to me a bit about the team that you're working with on this course.*

> Reality
> question 1

Pete: *There is a team of five permanent senior lecturers and three hourly paid lecturers who also contribute to modules – they're not permanent staff. But all of us have been involved with the course over a number of years. We've noticed that this feedback was particularly negative this year. And we think there were lots of factors contributing to that, including the impact of the pandemic and the move to online learning from face-to-face learning. This has affected course content and limited students' opportunities to work with external experts, and limited their opportunities to see how the theory applies to practice in the workplace.*

Sue: *Choose one of the feedback statements for us to start with.*

Pete: *I think I'd like to look at the student's point about some of the seminars being a waste of time: that students are left to work things out for themselves.*

> Reality
> question 2

Sue: *Can you share with me how these seminars were different to seminars before lockdown, before the pandemic?*

Pete: *In a way I don't think they were very different. I would have split the students into smaller groups to work collaboratively, to work out solutions to problems, for example. We did the same type of thing online: we had breakout rooms on Zoom. Then I'd bring them back together again – and actually what isn't coming across in the feedback is that students just wouldn't have anything to say. It was really … it is really a student problem. They just weren't engaging. That might have been to do with working online, of course.*

Pete implies that because these approaches had worked when seminars took place in-person, the ineffectiveness of employing the same approach when working online is *a student problem*. This suggests that Pete's evaluation is limited by functional fixedness (see Chapter 5).

Sue: *How do you think working online might influence the students' perception of the seminars?*

Pete: *I suppose, because of, you know, social media and all the time they spend on Facebook, I suppose, they're used to being passive participants. And being set activities to engage with online as a small group, maybe they're just used to being kind of passive with no one taking the lead. Whereas I think when we're together on campus, face to face, maybe there's more pressure, more peer expectation to participate more actively.*

Stereotyping (see Chapter 5) is present here. Pete has decided that the passivity he perceives is caused by student engagement with social media. We could also argue that this is indirectly evidence of the IKEA effect (see Chapter 2): Pete has decided that the activities created for students are effective – there is no reason why students shouldn't engage with them; students' lack of active engagement must be due to student deficiencies or failings.

> Sue seeks
> confirmation
> that this focus
> will be useful

Sue: *Before we think about how you could review working online, do you know whether the course will continue to use online platforms?*

Pete: *Yes, we're going for a hybrid model now, mixing the strongest elements of online learning with some on campus in-person interactions.*

Sue: *Imagine that I'd written this feedback. What would you want to say to me about how I might have engaged more fully in that seminar?*

Pete: *I'd want to say something to you about how, as you go through a university course, you have to understand that it's your responsibility to take more initiative. That's what university is about: it's about developing the type of graduate skills that you're going to need to have as a professional. And that means that you've got to be active and connect the dots really and work out for yourself how to make the most of the opportunities that we provide.*

It is possible that the Curse of Knowledge (see Chapter 5) is present here. In his own mind, Pete is clear about the developmental journey that undergraduates should make from the first year to completion. But it is not entirely clear that this expectation is clear to students,

Sue: *Do you have different expectations of students at different stages of the course?*

Pete: *Yes. I'd expect to need to provide much clearer guidance to first-year undergraduates, and I'd scaffold the process much more clearly. I would model what engagement with the activity would look like. I might get some students to volunteer to complete a short activity in front of the whole group and we would have a conversation about it with everybody. But by the third year I'd expect students to take that on themselves.*

Sue: *And is that in place at the moment? Is there scaffolding that you're aware of for first-year students?*

Pete: *Certainly: the team is clear about this sense of increasingly handing over own-ership and responsibility to students. Because in the third year, students will be writing their dissertations, carrying out independent research: it's really important for them to take ownership and responsibility.*

Pete's certainty that his team has shared expectations of students is possibly a positive, suggesting that students will receive a consistent message from lecturers. However, it also may suggest groupthink (see Chapter 4): a lack of divergent thinking around, in this case, student capacity to assume ownership and responsibility.

Sue: *Could members of the team share the strategies they've used successfully?*

Options
question 1

Pete: *To be honest, we're so stretched as a team.*

Options
question 2

Sue: *Okay. I wonder whether there's an opportunity to have a checklist or some guidance for lecturers teaching different modules. Maybe some guidance for lecturers shifting from teaching a first year to a third-year module?*

Pete: *I know what you mean. But I'd be concerned because this is a really experienced team. I wouldn't want them to feel that I was being condescending or, you know, telling them how to do their job. Because they know how to do it: they've been doing this for years. They know how to work with students. We've had really, really good feedback in previous years. This is a blip. They've taught really effectively for a long time and those approaches have always worked. Saying to them now, 'this is what you should be doing': it won't go down very well.*

Status quo bias (see Chapter 3) is clearly present here. The approaches the course team have used in the past have worked, at least in the sense that student evaluation of the course has been positive. Pete also appears to be concerned that challenging others or recommending approaches will unsettle the team.

Sue moves the dialogue in a different direction, focusing on what had worked when the seminars had been in-person and on campus. Pete notes that there had been informal opportunities for individual students to ask questions at the end of sessions. Sue suggests that that these one-to-one opportunities could be replicated online, with lecturers concluding the core content 10–15 minutes before the scheduled end time. Alternatively, students could be invited to contact lecturers during office hours. Pete remains concerned about workload, but sees that time allocated within the timetabled session could work.

Options
question 3

Sue: *I wonder whether there might be another opportunity here. If you kind of visualise them in a face-to-face context, what kind of messages and signals do you give them that maybe are not so easily replicated when working in Zoom and then being sent to breakout rooms?*

Pete: *When we were working in-person on campus and we've got different groups working on a problem-solving activity, for example, then it was very easy to manage. I could dip into what different groups were doing, and stop everybody and draw their attention to, you know, a particular group working in an interesting way, or thinking about the problem in a way that maybe was unexpected and I'd say, 'Can everyone stop – let's hear how this group are dealing with the problem'. That would potentially stimulate other groups or model a way of approaching the activity. But I've found that juggling between breakout groups and the whole group collectively is technically much harder.*

Sue acknowledges the additional technical challenge. Sue and Pete explore the duration of breakout activities and agree that 'chunking' or dividing longer activities into parts, with regular opportunities to return to the main group, could facilitate students' engagement.

Sue finishes the discussion by asking Pete to identify what he will take away from the meeting.

As exemplified in the dialogue, biases operate independently and enforce other biases. The strategies below identify ways that individuals working at different levels in HEIs can take responsibility and action.

Strategies to address interconnecting biases

At an individual level

Once we open our eyes to the prevalence of cognitive biases, we are primed to recognise them. While we cannot pre-empt unconscious biases, we can train ourselves to be more alert to the ones we recognise and to be watchful for others.

At a team level

Teacher teams aim to cultivate pedagogic and curricular practices, which best suit the needs of the students, the teachers and are compliant with institutional requirements. It is challenging to meet the needs of all stakeholders, to be aware of the influence of unconscious biases and to address the effects of conscious and unconscious biases. By including student partners and other external stakeholders in HE course evaluation, the increased diversity and increased watchfulness of those evaluating course design and delivery are more likely to offset the negative impacts of bias.

At an institutional level

HEIs develop and implement strategies to manage their large, often devolved enterprises. As employees, we trust that these strategies support good governance, quality assurance and well-being for students and staff. However, strategies are not necessarily quality assured for bias awareness. And individuals with diverse interests and responsibilities will interpret and implement these strategies in different ways. HEI executive teams need to nominate bias-aware ambassadors who critically evaluate institution-wide strategies and lead on any relevant action.

Concluding remarks

Through this book's six dialogues between HE lecturers, course leaders and educational developers, where the peer coach has applied tailored versions of the GROW coaching model, we have shared safe ways to discuss bias in HE. The GROW coaching model provides an accessible and intuitive structure which as shown can be adapted to support different levels of self-reflection. As illustrated in Table 1.1 (see Chapter 1), each chapter's dialogue elicits its own selection of cognitive biases, with some biases being revisited in different chapters. The book does not identify a comprehensive selection of biases and different coaching partners or coaching models may elicit alternative biases. However, we feel the selection discussed in this book is sufficiently representative of biases that can influence HE practices.

Raising awareness of conscious and where possible unconscious biases is a crucial first step. We need to know what has to be addressed, followed by strategies for effective action and follow-up. Each chapter provides a list of such strategies, many of which are taken from current HE practices which support inclusive course design and pedagogy. Through our further consideration of these strategies, we feel that their potential for addressing bias becomes evident. Lecturers, course leaders and educational developers are all ideally placed to implement and evaluate the impact of bias-addressing strategies in HE teaching, learning and assessment. However, if we are to address bias systemically then, as discussed in Chapter 6, individual actions are not enough. Individuals have agency and arguably we have greatest impact when we collaborate within and across our HE institutions. It falls to individuals to hold their HEIs accountable and to actively pursue equity, inclusion and equality of opportunity for all. Our hope is that our book signals that dialogic openness and reflectiveness are important pre-cursors for developing awareness of bias, and that there is a wealth of strategies and actions for addressing bias at individual, team and institutional levels. With commitment and strategic action we will move forward in addressing bias.

Critical questions for practice

» What do we each do to support and develop our bias watchfulness?

» How do we assure students that we take issues concerning bias seriously?

» How do we benefit from sharing our bias-aware practices?

» What do our teams have in place that specifically supports the pursuit of unbiased pedagogic practices and curricular content?

» How do our HEIs evaluate institutional strategies for bias?

» Who holds each HEI accountable for identifying and addressing bias?

Summary

- Module, course or departmental management responsibility will bring with it interconnecting challenges and biases.

- Our response to Covid-19 has involved a shift to a greater or lesser extent to online learning and teaching. Where online approaches are retained, our assumptions about 'what works' require examination.

- The more we recognise the prevalence of biases, the better equipped we are to address these and provide an experience for all characterised by social justice.

Useful links

Equality and Human Rights Commission – Promoting and upholding equality and human rights ideals and laws across England, Scotland and Wales. [online] Available at: www.equalityhumanrights.com/en (accessed 13 January 2022).

The Equality and Human Rights Commission provides expert information and legal guidance on equality and human rights within Britain. The site includes a hotline for advice and support on discrimination.

Runnymede – Intelligence for a Multiethnic Britain. [online] Available at: www. runnymedetrust.org/ (accessed 13 January 2022).

The Runnymede Trust has existed since 1968 and is committed to achieving an inclusive multicultural Britain. Through the website you can access resources, publications and information on their projects.

References

Adams, Richard (2020) Fewer than 1 of UK University Professors are Black – Figures Show. [online] Available at: www.theguardian.com/education/2020/feb/27/fewer-than-1-of-uk-university-professors-are-black-figures-show (accessed 13 January 2022).

Akinbode, Adenike (2015) The Quiet Learner and the Quiet Teacher. *Link*, 1(2). [online] Available at: www.herts.ac.uk/link/volume-1,-issue-2/the-quiet-learner-and-the-quiet-teacher (accessed 26 January 2022).

Alexander, Claire (2017) Breaking Black: The Death of Ethnic and Racial Studies in Britain. *Ethnic and Racial Studies*, 41(6): 1034–54.

Alexander, Claire and **Arday**, Jason (eds) (2015) *Aiming Higher: Race, Inequality and Diversity in the Academy*. London: Runnymede Trust. [online] Available at: www.runnymedetrust.org/uploads/Aiming%20Higher.pdf (accessed 13 January 2022).

Allport, Gordon (1954/1979) *The Nature of Prejudice*. Cambridge, MA: Perseus.

Amos, Valerie and **Doku**, Amatey (2019a) Black, Asian and Minority Ethnic Student Attainment at UK Universities: Closing the Gap. [online] Available at: www.universitiesuk.ac.uk/policy-and-analysis/reports/Pages/bame-student-attainment-uk-universities-closing-the-gap.aspx (accessed 13 January 2022).

Amos, Valerie and **Doku**, Amatey (2019b) Black, Asian and Minority Ethnic Student Attainment at UK Universities: #Closing the Gap. Case Studies. [online] Available at: www.universitiesuk.ac.uk/sites/default/files/field/downloads/2021-09/bame-student-attainment-uk-universities-case-studies.pdf (accessed 13 January 2022).

Anderson, Lorin W; **Krathwohl**, David R; **Airasian**, Peter W; **Cruikshank**, Kathleen A; **Mayer**, Richard E; **Pintrich**, Paul R; **Raths**, James and **Wittrock**, Merlin C (2001) *A Taxonomy for Learning, Teaching, and Assessing: A Revision of Bloom's Taxonomy of Educational Objectives*. New York: Longman.

Arday, Jason (2015) Creating Space and Providing Opportunities for BME Academics in Higher Education. In **Alexander**, Claire and **Arday**, Jason (eds) *Aiming Higher: Race, Inequality and Diversity in the Academy* (pp 40–2). Runnymede Perspectives. London: Runnymede.

Argyris, Chris (1977) Double Loop Learning in Organizations. *Harvard Business Review*. [online] Available at: https://hbr.org/1977/09/double-loop-learning-in-organizations (accessed 13 January 2022).

Atewologun, Doyin; **Cornish**, Tinu and **Tresh**, Fatima (2018) Unconscious Bias Training: An Assessment of the Evidence for Effectiveness. Equality and Human Rights Commission, UK. [online] Available at: www.equalityhumanrights.com (accessed 13 January 2022).

Azumah Dennis, Carol (2018) Decolonising Education: A Pedagogic Intervention. In **Bhambra**, Gurminder K; **Gebrial**, Dalia and **Nişancıoğlu**, Kerem (eds) *Decolonising the University Curriculum* (pp 190–207). London: Pluto Press.

Bandura, Albert (1977) Self-efficacy: Toward a Unifying Theory of Behavioral Change. *Psychological Review*, 84(2): 191–215.

Batten, John; **Bateya**, Jo; **Shafea**, Laura; **Gubby**, Laura and **Birch**, Phil (2013) The Influence of Reputation Information on the Assessment of Undergraduate Student Work. *Assessment & Evaluation in Higher Education*, 38(4): 417–35.

Benson, Buster (2016) Cognitive Bias Codex. [online] Available at: https://busterbenson.com/piles/cognitive-biases/ (accessed 13 January 2022).

Bhambra, Gurminder K; **Gebrial**, Dalia and **Nişancıoğlu**, Kerem (eds) (2018) *Decolonising the University Curriculum*. London: Pluto Press.

Biggs, John (1996) Enhancing Teaching Through Constructive Alignment. *Higher Education*, 32: 347–64.

Biggs, John and **Collis**, Kevin (1982) *Evaluating the Quality of Learning: The SOLO Taxonomy.* New York: Academic.

Biggs, John and **Tang**, Catherine (2007) Designing Intended Learning Outcomes. In **Biggs**, John and **Tang**, Catherine (eds) *Teaching for Quality Learning at University.* 3rd ed (pp 64–90). Milton Keynes: Oxford University Press.

Bloxham, Susan and **Price**, Margaret (2015) External Examining: Fit for Purpose? *Studies in Higher Education*, 40(2): 195–211.

Bloxham, Sue; **Boyd**, Peter and **Orr**, Susan (2011) Mark My Words: The Role of Assessment Criteria in UK Higher Education Grading Practices. *Studies in Higher Education*, 36(6): 655–70.

Bovill, Cathy (2020) *Co-creating Learning and Teaching. Towards Relational Pedagogy in Higher Education.* London: Critical Publishing.

British Educational Research Association (2019) Ethical Guidelines for Educational Research, fourth edition. [online] Available at: www.bera.ac.uk/publication/ethical-guidelines-for-educational-research-2018-online#consent (accessed 4 February 2022).

Burgstahler, Sheryl (2021) Universal Design in Education: Principles and Applications, Disabilities, Opportunities, Internetworking, and Technology. [online] Available at: www.washington.edu/doit/sites/default/files/atoms/files/UDE-Principles-and-Applications.pdf (accessed 12 January 2022).

Centre for Teaching and Learning, University of Southern Denmark (2016) Internationalising the Curriculum, Developing Students Intercultural Competencies. Video – Intercultural Group Work Role Play. [online] Available at: https://itc.sdu.dk/index.php?page=1.-enabling-intercultural-group-work (accessed 12 January 2022).

Corbyn, Zoë (2021) Microsoft's Kate Crawford: 'AI is Neither Artificial nor Intelligent'. [online] Available at: www.theguardian.com/technology/2021/jun/06/microsofts-kate-crawford-ai-is-neither-artificial-nor-intelligent (accessed 13 January 2022).

Dacre Pool, Lorraine and **Sewell**, Peter (2007) The Key to Employability: Developing a Practical Model of Graduate Employability. *Education+Training*, 49(4): 277–89.

Dastin, Jeffery (2018) Amazon Scraps Secret AI Recruiting Tool that Showed Bias Against Women. *Reuters*. [online] Available at: www.reuters.com/article/us-amazon-com-jobs-automation-insight-idUSKCN1MK08G (accessed 13 January 2022).

de Bono, Edward (1985) *Six Thinking Hats: An Essential Approach to Business Management.* London: Penguin.

Department for Education (2014) The National Curriculum in England, Framework document. [online] Available at: https://assets.publishing.service.gov.uk/government/uploads/system/uploads/attachment_data/file/381344/Master_final_national_curriculum_28_Nov.pdf (accessed 13 January 2022).

Donovan, Joan; **Caplan**, Robyn; **Matthews**, Jeanna and **Hansen**, Lauren (2018) Algorithmic Accountability: A Primer. Tech Algorithm Briefing: How Algorithms Perpetuate Racial Bias and Inequality. *Data and Society.* [online] Available at: https://datasociety.net/library/algorithmic-accountability-a-primer/ (accessed 13 January 2022).

Dweck, Carol S (2006) *Mindset: The New Psychology of Success.* New York: Ballantine Books.

Ecclestone, Kathryn (2001) I Know a 2:1 When I See It: Understanding Criteria for Degree Classifications in Franchised University Programmes. *Journal of Further and Higher Education*, 25(3): 301–13.

Educational Quality at Universities for Inclusive International Programmes (EQUiiP) (2019) *The Role of Language in the International Classroom.* [online] Available at: https://equiip.eu/module/language/ (accessed 13 January 2022).

Eisner, Elliot W (1985) *The Art of Educational Evaluation: A Personal View.* London: Falmer Press.

Fung, Dilly (2017) A Connected Curriculum for Higher Education. [online] Available at: https://discovery.ucl.ac.uk/id/eprint/1558776/1/A-Connected-Curriculum-for-Higher-Education.pdf (accessed 12 January 2022).

Galinsky, Adam D; **Todd**, Andrew R; **Homan**, Astrid C; **Phillips**, Katherine W; **Apfelbaum**, Evan P; **Sasaki**, Stacey J and **Maddux**, William W (2015) Maximizing the Gains and Minimizing the Pains of Diversity: A Policy Perspective. *Perspectives on Psychological Science*, 10(6): 742–8.

Gandolfi, Heira (2021) Decolonising the Science Curriculum in England: Bringing Decolonial Science and Technology Studies to Secondary Education. *The Curriculum Journal*, 32: 510–32.

Gladwell, Malcolm (2008) *Outliers: The Story of Success.* London: Penguin.

Gourlay, Lesley (2015) 'Student Engagement' and the Tyranny of Participation. *Teaching in Higher Education*, 20(4): 402–11.

Gupta, Manjul; **Parra**, Carlos and **Dennehy**, Denis (2021) Questioning Racial and Gender Bias in AI-based Recommendations: Do Espoused National Cultural Values Matter? *Information Systems Frontiers*. [online] Available at: https://link.springer.com/article/10.1007/s10796-021-10156-2 (accessed 8 March 2022).

Harris, Jenine K; **Croston**, Meriah A; **Hutti**, Ellen T and **Eyler**, Amy A (2020) Diversify the Syllabi: Underrepresentation of Female Authors in College Course Readings. *PLoS ONE*, 15(10): e0239012. [online] Available at: https://journals.plos.org/plosone/article?id=10.1371/journal.pone.0239012 (accessed 18 January 2022).

Harrison, Neil (2012) Investigating the Impact of Personality and Early Life Experiences on Intercultural Interaction in Internationalised Universities. *International Journal of Intercultural Relations*, 36: 224–37.

Hazen, Helen (2020) Use of Oral Examinations to Assess Student Learning in the Social Sciences. *Journal of Geography in Higher Education*, 44(4): 592–607.

Henderson, Morag; **Shure**, Nikki and **Adamecz-Völgyi**, Anna (2020) Moving on Up: 'First in Family' University Graduates in England. *Oxford Review of Education*, 46(6): 734–51.

Higbee, Jeanne (2017) The Faculty Perspective: Implementation of Universal Design in a First-Year Classroom. In **Burgstahler**, Sheryl (ed) *Universal Design in Higher Education: From Principles to Practice* (pp 61–72). Cambridge, MA: Harvard University Press.

Higher Education Statistics Agency (2021) Who's Working in HE? [online] Available at: www.hesa.ac.uk/data-and-analysis/staff/working-in-he (accessed 13 January 2022).

Hinton, Daniel P and **Higson**, Helen (2017) A Large-Scale Examination of the Effectiveness of Anonymous Marking in Reducing Group Performance Differences in Higher Education Assessment. *PLoS ONE*, 12(8): e0182711. [online] Available at: https://journals.plos.org/plosone/article?id=10.1371/journal.pone.0182711 (accessed 13 January 2022).

Hockings, Christine (2010) Inclusive Teaching and Learning in Higher Education: A Synthesis of Research. [online] Available at: www.advance-he.ac.uk/knowledge-hub/inclusive-learning-and-teaching-higher-education-synthesis-research (accessed 13 January 2022).

Hurford, Donna (2020) DUT Guide: Strategies for Criteria-aligned, Fair and Inclusive Oral Exams. *Dansk Universitetspædagogisk Tidsskrift*. Årgang 16 nr. 29/2020. [online] Available at: https://dun-net.dk/media/1438794/dut_29_hurford_dut_guide_strategies_for_criteria-aligned_fair_and_inclusive.pdf (accessed 13 January 2022).

Hussey, Trevor and **Smith**, Patrick (2003) The Trouble with Learning Outcomes. *Active Learning in Higher Education*, 3(3): 220–33.

Inan-Kaya, Gamze and **Rubie-Davies**, Christine (2021) Teacher Classroom Interactions and Behaviours: Indications of Bias. *Learning and Instruction*. [online] Available at: https://doi.org/10.1016/j.learninstruc.2021.101516 (accessed 12 January 2022).

Jæger, Kirsten and **Gram**, Malene (2015) (Self)Confidence or Compliance Students' Experience of Academic Quality in Study-Abroad Contexts. *Learning and Teaching*, 8(3): 37–59.

Johnson, David W; **Johnson**, Roger T and **Smith**, Karl A (2014) Cooperative Learning: Improving University Instruction by Basing Practice on Validated Theory. *Journal on Excellence in College Teaching*, 25(3–4): 85–118.

Kahneman, Daniel (2011) *Thinking, Fast and Slow*. London: Penguin.

Kara, Helen (2020) Decolonising Methods: A Reading List. [online] Available at: https://helenkara.com/2020/07/29/decolonising-methods-a-reading-list/ (accessed 13 January 2022).

Killick, David (2015a) *Developing the Global Student. Higher Education in an Era of Globalization*. London: Routledge.

Killick, David (2015b) Internationalisation and the Academic Developer. *Educational Developments*, 16(3): 1–6. [online] Available at: www.seda.ac.uk/seda-publishing/educational-developments/past-issues-2000-onwards/educational-developments-issue-16-3-2015/ (accessed 13 January 2022).

Killick, David and **Foster**, Monika (2021) *Learner Relationships in Global Higher Education*. London: Routledge.

Lawlor, K Blaine and **Hornyak**, Martyn (2012) Smart Goals: How the Application of Smart Goals Can Contribute to Achievement of Student Learning Outcomes. *Developments in Business Simulation and Experiential Learning*, 39: 259–67.

MacMullen, Ian (2011) On Status Quo Bias in Civic Education. *The Journal of Politics*, 73(3): 872–86.

Malouff, John and **Thorsteinsson**, Einer B (2016) Bias in Grading: 'A Meta-Analysis of Experimental Research Findings.' *Australian Journal of Education*, 60(3): 245–56.

Mansfield, Andrew (2019) Confusion, Contradiction and Exclusion: The Promotion of British Values in the Teaching of History in Schools. *The Curriculum Journal*, 30(1): 40–50.

Manz, Charles C and **Neck**, Christopher P (1995) Team Think: Beyond the Group Think Syndrome in Self-managing Work Teams. *Journal of Managerial Psychology*, 10(1): 7–15.

Marsh, Lauren; **Kanngiesser**, Patricia and **Hood**, Bruce (2018) When and How Does Labour Lead to Love? The Ontogeny and Mechanisms of the IKEA Effect. *Cognition*, 170: 245–53.

Martin, Nicola; **Wray**, Michael; **James**, Abi; **Draffan**, E A; **Krupa**, Joanna and **Turner**, Paddy (2019) *Implementing Inclusive Teaching and Learning in UK Higher Education – Utilising Universal Design for Learning (UDL) as a Route to Excellence*. London: Society for Research into Higher Education.

Marton, Ference and **Säljö**, Roger (1997) 'Chapter 3: Approaches to Learning'. In Marton, Ference; Hounsell, Dai and Entwistle, Noel (eds) *The Experience of Learning* (pp 39–58). Edinburgh: Scottish Academic Press.

McConlogue, Teresa (2020) *Assessment and Feedback in Higher Education – A Guide for Teachers*. London: UCL Press.

McGarr, Olliver and **Clifford**, Amanda Marie (2013) Just Enough to Make You Take It Seriously: Exploring Students' Attitudes Towards Peer Assessment. *Higher Education*, 65(6): 677–93.

Merry, Kevin (2021) Universal Design for Learning: An Antidote to Digital Poverty. *AdvanceHE*, April 14. [online] Available at: www.advance-he.ac.uk/news-and-views/universal-design-learning-antidote-digital-poverty (accessed 13 January 2022).

Meyer, Jan and **Land**, Ray (2003) Threshold Concepts and Troublesome Knowledge: Linkages to Ways of Thinking and Practising within the Disciplines. Occasional Report 4, May. Edinburgh: Enhancing Teaching-Learning Environments in Undergraduate Courses Project.

Mnasri, Salaheddine and **Papakonstantinidis**, Stavros (2020) Detrivialisation as a Strategy to Challenge Organisational Groupthink. *The Electronic Journal of Knowledge Management*, 18(3): 224–35. [online] Available at: https://academic-publishing.org/index.php/ejkm/article/view/1157 (accessed 13 January 2022).

Moreno, Jacob (1934) *Who Shall Survive?* Boston, MA: Beacon House.

Moss-Racusin, Corinne A; **Dovidio**, John F; **Brescoll**, Victoria L; **Graham**, Mark J and **Handelsman**, Jo (2012) Science Faculty's Subtle Gender Biases Favor Male Students. *PNAS*, 109(41): 16474–9.

Munch-Jurisic, Ditte Marie (2020) The Right to Feel Comfortable: Implicit Bias and the Moral Potential of Discomfort. *Ethical Theory and Moral Practice*, 23: 237–50.

Noon, Mike (2018) Pointless Diversity Training: Unconscious Bias, New Racism and Agency. *Work, Employment and Society*, 32(1):198–209.

Organisation for Economic Co-operation and Development (OECD) (2019) Transformative Competencies for 2030. [online] Available at: www.oecd.org/education/2030-project/teaching-and-learning/learning/transformative-competencies/Transformative_Competencies_for_2030_concept_note.pdf (accessed 13 January 2022).

Otting, Hans; **Zwaal**, Wichard; **Tempelaar**, Dirk and **Gijselaers**, Wim (2010) The Structural Relationship Between Students' Epistemological Beliefs and Conceptions of Teaching and Learning. *Studies in Higher Education*, 35(7): 741–60.

Oxfam (2015) Global Citizenship in the Classroom – A Guide for Teachers. [online] Available at: https://oxfamilibrary.openrepository.com/bitstream/handle/10546/620105/edu-global-citizenship-teacher-guide-091115-en.pdf?sequence=9&isAllowed=y (accessed 13 January 2022).

Palluck, Elizabeth L and **Green**, Donald P (2009) Prejudice Reduction: What Works? A Review and Assessment of Research and Practice. *Annual Review of Psychology*, 60: 339–67.

Phillips, Katherine W; **Northcraft**, Gregory B and **Neale**, Margaret A (2006) Surface-Level Diversity and Decision-Making in Groups: When Does Deep-Level Similarity Help? *Group Processes & Intergroup Relations*, 9(4): 467–82.

Phull, Kiran; **Ciflikli**, Gokhan and **Meibauer**, Gustav (2019) Gender and Bias in the International Relations Curriculum: Insights from Reading Lists. *European Journal of International Relations*, 25(2): 383–407.

Pilkington, Andrew (2018) The Rise and Fall in the Salience of Race Equality in Higher Education. In **Arday**, Jason and **Mirza**, Heidi Safa (eds) *Dismantling Race in Higher Education Racism, Whiteness and Decolonising the Academy* (pp 27–45). London: Palgrave.

Pinker, Steven (2015) *The Sense of Style: The Thinking Person's Guide to Writing in the 21st Century.* London: Penguin.

Pitt, Edd and **Winstone**, Naomi (2018) The Impact of Anonymous Marking on Students' Perceptions of Fairness, Feedback and Relationships with Lecturers. *Assessment & Evaluation in Higher Education*, 43(7): 1183–93.

Poce, Antonella; **Amenduni**, Francesca and **De Medio**, Carlo (2019) From Tinkering to Thinkering: Tinkering as Critical and Creative Thinking Enhancer. *Journal of e-Learning and Knowledge Society*, 15(2): 101–12.

Prescod-Weinstein, Chanda (2015) Decolonising Science Reading List. It's the End of Science as You Know It. [online] Available at: https://medium.com/@chanda/decolonising-science-reading-list-339fb773d51f (accessed 13 January 2022).

Pronin, Emily; **Gilovich**, Thomas and **Ross**, Lee (2004) Objectivity in the Eye of the Beholder: Divergent Perceptions of Bias in Self Versus Others. *Psychological Review*, 111(3): 781–99.

Pronin, Emily and **Kugler**, Matthew B (2007) Valuing Thoughts, Ignoring Behavior: The Introspection Illusion as a Source of the Bias Blind Spot. *Journal of Experimental Psychology*, 43: 565–78.

Read, Andrew and **Hurford**, Donna (2010) 'I Know How to Read Longer Novels': Developing Pupils' Success Criteria in the Classroom. *Education 3–13 International Journal of Primary, Elementary and Early Years Education*, 38(1): 87–100.

Reay, Diane (2018) Race and Elite Universities in the UK. In **Arday**, Jason and **Mirza**, Heidi Safa (eds) *Dismantling Race in Higher Education Racism, Whiteness and Decolonising the Academy* (pp 47–66). London: Palgrave.

Resnick, Mitchel and **Rosenbaum**, Eric (2013) Designing for Tinkerability. In **Kanter**, David and **Honey**, Margaret (eds) *Design, Make, Play: Growing the Next Generation of STEM Innovators* (pp 163–81). Abingdon: Taylor & Francis.

Roberts, Celia; **Sarangi**, Srikant; **Southgate**, Lesley; **Wakeford**, Richard and **Wass**, Val (2000) Oral Examinations – Equal Opportunities, Ethnicity, and Fairness in the MRCGP. *British Medical Journal*, 320(5): 370–4.

Sadler, D Royce (2005) Interpretations of Criteria-based Assessment and Grading in Higher Education. *Assessment and Evaluation in Higher Education*, 30(2): 175–94.

Schön, Donald (1987) *Educating the Reflective Practitioner: Toward a New Design for Teaching and Learning in the Professions*. San Francisco, CA: Jossey-Bass.

Schucan Bird, Karen and **Pitman**, Lesley (2020) How Diverse Is Your Reading List? Exploring Issues of Representation and Decolonisation in the UK. *Higher Education*, 79: 903–20.

Slavin, Robert E (2014) Cooperative Learning and Academic Achievement: Why Does Groupwork Work? *Anales de psicologia*, 30(3): 785–91.

Spencer-Oatey, Helen and **Stadler**, Stefanie (2009) The Global People Competency Framework. Competencies for Effective Intercultural Interaction. The Centre for Applied Linguistics, University of Warwick. [online] Available at: https://core.ac.uk/download/pdf/46445.pdf (accessed 13 January 2022).

Spowart, Nan (2017) Profile: Antonio Guterres. *The National*, 3 January. [online] Available at: www.thenational.scot/news/14998151.profile-antonio-guterres/ (accessed 13 January 2022).

Tange, Hanne and **Millar**, Sharon (2016) Opening the Mind? Geographies of Knowledge and Curricular Practices. *Higher Education*, 72: 573–87.

The Warwick Commission (2015) *Enriching Britain: Culture, Creativity and Growth*. The 2015 Report by the Warwick Commission on the Future of Cultural Value. University of Warwick, Coventry, UK. [online] Available at: https://warwick.ac.uk/research/warwickcommission/futureculture/finalreport/ (accessed 13 January 2022).

Tversky, Amos and **Kahneman**, Daniel (1974) Judgment under Uncertainty: Heuristics and Biases. *Science, New Series*, 185(4157): 1124–31.

Ulriksen, Lars (2009) The Implied Student. *Studies in Higher Education*, 34(5): 517–32.

University of Arts, London (nd) Decolonising Reading Lists. [online] Available at: www.arts.ac.uk/_data/assets/pdf_file/0021/201936/Decolonising-reading-lists-PDF-703KB.pdf (accessed 12 January 2022).

University College London (nd) Inclusive Curriculum Health Check. [online] Available at: www.ucl.ac.uk/teaching-learning/sites/teaching-learning/files/ucl_inclusive_curriculum_healthcheck_2018.pdf (accessed 13 January 2022).

University of Hertfordshire (nd) Equality Diversity and Inclusion: Resources for Facilitating Conversations and Learning. [online] Available at: www.herts.ac.uk/study/schools-of-study/education/research/FLiTE/flite-resources (accessed 26 January 2022).

University of Huddersfield (nd) Reading List Toolkit. Broaden My Bookshelf. [online] Available at: https://hud.libguides.com/c.php?g=679688&p=4850462 (accessed 13 January 2022).

University of Westminster (nd) Reading Lists. Pedagogies for Social Justice. [online] Available at: http://blog.westminster.ac.uk/psj/tools/reading-lists/ (accessed 13 January 2022).

Whitmore, John (2017) *Coaching for Performance: The Principles and Practice of Coaching and Leadership*. 5th ed. Boston, MA: Nicholas Brealey Publishing.

Zahra, Daniel; **Robinson**, Iain; **Roberts**, Martin; **Coombes**, Lee; **Cockerill**, Josephine and **Burr**, Steven (2017) Rigour in Moderation Processes Is More Important than the Choice of Method. *Assessment & Evaluation in Higher Education*, 42(7): 1159–67.

Zalewski, Andrzej; **Borowa**, Klara and **Ratkowski**, Andrzej (2017) On Cognitive Biases in Architecture Decision Making. In **Lopes**, Antonia and **de Lemos**, Rogério (eds) *Software Architecture. ECSA 2017. Lecture Notes in Computer Science*, 10475: 3–21. Cham: Springer.

Zhu, Chuanyan and **Gao**, Yun (2012) Communication with Chinese International Students: Understanding Chinese International Students' Learning Difficulties and Communication Barriers. Paper presented at the British Educational Research Association Annual Conference, University of Manchester, UK. 4–6 September 2012.

Index